Three Score Years and Twenty

Walter soon after his arrival in Australia in 1938.

Three Score Years and Twenty

WALTER C. BALMFORD O.B.E., F.I.A.

EDITORS
JOHN D. BALMFORD
CHRISTOPHER J. BALMFORD

ARCADIA

First published 2019 by ARCADIA
the general books' imprint of
Australian Scholarly Publishing Pty Ltd
7 Lt Lothian St Nth, North Melbourne, Vic 3051
Tel: 03 9329 6963 / Fax: 03 9329 5452
enquiry@scholarly.info / www.scholarly.info

ISBN 978-1-925801-77-4

Cover design: Wayne Saunders

All images on cover, and most images in text, photographed (or scanned) by Lauren Dunn. Exceptions (the photos of Arnie) scanned by David Balmford.

Contents

Introduction

My father, Walter Balmford, always said that he would retire when he was sixty, not at 65 as was more usual at the time. Apart from his service in World War One, he had spent his working life practising as an actuary – as a Civil Servant in London, until 1938 – and as a Public Servant in Canberra, from 1938 until retirement in 1958, aged 62. He stayed on for two years longer than he planned because there were a few things he wanted to finish, he said.

As he approached 80, his lifelong English friend, Sir Harold Emmerson, himself a distinguished Civil Servant, presented an early draft of his own memoirs for comment on his recollections of his (and their) early life.

It was that event which prompted my father to take up his own pen and start to write, literally. No personal computer of course, although I remember him telling me that his office, that of Commonwealth Actuary, now that of the Australian Government Actuary, had the first computer in the Commonwealth Public Service, it no doubt being essential for preparation of the Australian Life Tables published under his name in 1948.

In his Foreword (1976), he expressly states that his memoirs should never be widely circulated – but over 40 years have now passed and his reasons no longer seem relevant.

On completion, he did arrange for a copy to be provided to the National Library in Canberra and to other appropriate bodies.

After his death, my late brother, Peter, and I circulated copies a little more widely, for they were, so we thought, of considerable historical interest in regard to two periods. His time in the Royal Flying Corps and Royal Air Force during World War One, and his working life in Australia, from shortly before World War Two until his retirement in 1958.

John D Balmford
May 2019

Foreword

Some of the few people who may read these memoirs may wonder why on earth I should want to write them. Let me assure all readers, at the outset, that the memoirs have not been written with a view to publication. Indeed they should never be widely circulated because some of my remarks about living people may cause distress, while others may provoke legal action. I wish neither event to occur.* I do not suffer any illusion that the story of my life could be of interest to anybody but myself, which words probably reveal my secret desire to relive some of the enjoyment I have had out of life. I do not delude myself that I have made any significant contribution to the common weal or have attained any eminent status. What has prompted me to tackle this job is the thought that I never met any of my grandparents and that I have often wondered what sort of a life they led. I do not know whether any of my descendants will have similar wonderings about me; anyway I will have done my best to help them. To perform this task I have done some research in encyclopaedias, atlases and numerous other reference books to check some of my statements. I kept a diary from 1916 to 1922 but – in a weak moment – when I read it for the first time in 1957, I burnt it because it seemed so utterly puerile. My main source of reference for the First World War has been my Pilot's Log Book. I have got a good memory for happenings in the distant past even if my family consider it a bit weak on recent events. At the moment I am within a few days of

* Editors: As explained in John D Balmford's Introduction, Walter's reasons for this concern have long since become irrelevant.

my 80th birthday and that is where my story ends but not before sending affectionate greetings to any of my descendants who may happen to read through these pages. In fact I dedicate the whole thing to them.

I have spread my dreams under your feet
Tread softly because you tread on my dreams

W.B. Yeats

Melbourne
August, 1976
Walter C. Balmford

Postscript

I hope my readers will agree with me when I say that I believe Saki was wrong on both counts when he wrote:

> The young have aspirations that never come to pass, the old have reminiscences of what never happened.

W.C.B.

Introduction

My intention in writing these memoirs is that they should be for the benefit of my descendants. Before starting on the part I know most about, namely my own life story, I will deal with the early history of the Balmfords, so far as it is known to me. I have always understood that they have been mainly associated with the West Riding of Yorkshire. I have also thought that the surname was uncommon, so it was a surprise to find the frequency of its occurrence in the records at Somerset House, London. Without employing a professional genealogist it is difficult for an amateur to trace his more remote ancestors, especially as the records in Somerset House do not include pre-1847 data. To investigate earlier years one has to use considerable imagination to find likely sources of information other than parish registers. As a basis for my records my Father, at the age of 84, prepared a complete family tree starting with my great grandfather, John, born in 1809. I failed to trace anyone earlier. Then, in 1964, I received a letter from Birmingham on the envelope of which was printed 'Walter Balmford Ltd'. This was something of a shock because I thought I was the one and only Walter Balmford. My correspondent and his Father were both named 'Walter' and they also thought that they were exceptional. I met both Walter Senior and Walter Junior in 1966. Walter Junior traced his ancestry back to James, born in the 1790's. Since then we have endeavoured to ascertain if and how we are related. I think Walter Junior has found the solution.* We discovered that both our families had been associated with Elland and Halifax in Yorkshire. So he visited both places and searched through the parish registers.

* Editors: There is an updated, and more accurate, family tree in Appendix D.

I reproduce in Appendix 'A' a simplified version of the two family trees. Walter Junior's great discovery was of John, born in 1769. He proved to be the father of two sons from whom our two families are descended. We are not absolutely certain whether we can claim the two Jacobi and Abraham as ancestors. The difficulty seems to be that two or three hundred years ago people did not always know how to spell their names. The recorders of the various events presumably wrote down what they thought the names sounded like. For instance Jacobus II is recorded under the surname Baumforth.

I do not know whether we will search any further. The records of Christian names and dates of birth do not tell us anything at all about what the people were like. I think however, that I have gained a little insight into the characters of some early Balmfords from my researches in the Reading Room of the British Museum. I found the names of six authors named Balmford. To my astonishment my own name was recorded as the author of a report describing my construction of a Life Table based on the results of an Australian Census. The name of my Father's brother, John Alfred, was also there. He was a Chartered Accountant who wrote a book about his 'Theory of Draughts'.

The details about the other three authors named Balmford are given in Appendix 'B', I have no idea whether these particular men were ancestors of mine. I did examine several of their books. They all seemed to contain the outpourings of people who today would be regarded as religious cranks.

~

I now proceed to deal with the more recent Balmfords.

My parents showed considerable felicity in their choice (if it were choice) of the dates of birth of at any rate three of their four children. I arrived on 28th August 1896, one day before the first anniversary of their wedding. Their second child, Ruth, was born on 31st December 1897, the thirtieth anniversary of my Father's birth. I can't find anything to associate with the birth of their third child, Marie, but when she died at the early age of four in 1903 their fourth child Olive, arrived a few days later on 8th August much to the comfort of my mother. All four children were born in Warrington, Lancashire, where I lived until the age of 18. My earliest recollection is from the days when I was put to bed for a while every afternoon. I suppose I was about three and I remember wishing, as I lay in bed, that I was a big boy of seven.

I said in the Foreword that I never met any of my grandparents. My maternal grandfather died when my mother was a very young child. I believe her mother did see me once before I was one year old. As for my paternal grandfather I sometimes cause peoples' eyebrows to raise by telling them that he died on the day after he was married. They raise them still further when I add that his six sons reached manhood. He was of course married twice. At the time of his death he was on his way to see me at the age of three months and had called to see another son, my favourite uncle James Edward. He died while my uncle was showing him around the Art Gallery and School of Art at Morecambe, Lancashire, where my uncle was a teacher. Actually Uncle Jimmie was a house painter who developed an interest in the more artistic side of the craft, studied at the art school and eventually became a part time teacher there. About 1905 he sold his painting business and entered into partnership with my Father. He came to live in our house in Warrington and continued to do so until he married about five years later. He brought with him some striking framed pictures which he had done himself. They were mostly charcoal or pencil drawings of geometrical models and what must have been ornamental plaster casts. I think it was the light and shade he had worked into them that made them so attractive. They were hanging on the walls of our large dining room and people who came to the house had never seen anything like them before. Many years ago my Uncle promised, at my request, to bequeath some of these fascinating pictures to me but he evidently forgot to do so even though I got a moderate monetary bequest from him.

My Mother had been brought up as a Methodist but after she married she attended the Baptist chapel in Warrington of which Father was a nominal member and which I was later to attend. Unlike me today, my Mother was deeply religious. She was a very hard worker and devoted to the welfare of her family. They were her first thoughts. She was a wowser as regards liquor almost to the end of her life although in her later years she was known to have a drop of port occasionally. I know she was an extremely honest woman even when she would have been well advised to tell a white lie. She once said to me 'I have never told a lie in my life' and did not like my boyish humour when I said 'I think that must be at least the second'. As her father had died when she was a very young child the family had a very hard time. My grandmother went to work in a woollen mill to get some sort of income to keep the family alive. And my Mother herself went to work at the same place as soon as she reached the age of 14. I don't think my mother ever told me any details of what life was like either at home or at work. She had had hardly any education, which was really a handicap to her in later life even though she had a lively mind. I shall always remember her with affection.

Although I had a real affection for my Father I have to admit that it was qualified in some ways. He had some real faults which he knew about and even tried to correct. I think I suffered as a result more than any other member of the family. He was very short-tempered and vented his spleen on me if I had done anything to offend him. I suppose I was a difficult child but I still don't think he had the right to suppress any views I might wish to express. I think his treatment set me back in my relations with other people in my early life. At any rate it taught me one thing, to give my own children complete freedom of speech. He was irascible which resulted in me having many thrashings. Another extraordinary piece of behaviour was that in an argument (either with me or even with his friends) he would hold forth and expound his views and then, if the other party tried to express his disagreement, he would exclaim 'That's all there is to it. I have said what I think and I don't want to hear any more about it'.

Perhaps I have remembered too vividly these unpleasant facts about him. At other times and certainly much more frequently he was all that a father should be. He would do anything for us as long as we behaved. He was extremely thoughtful and kind. In order to illustrate both these facets of his behaviour I will recount some of the incidents of my early life.

One day when Ruth and I went to Manchester with him he took us to an expensive restaurant and gave us a good meal. Afterwards when walking down the street he said in front of some building 'I think we will go in here'.

We were led into the place among a crowd of people and after climbing some stairs, entered into what was the front row of the dress circle in a theatre. Ruth and I had never been to a theatre before. I don't think we had any idea of what was going to happen. Nor do I think that we realized that he had booked the seats earlier in the morning. It was a Christmas Pantomine – Cinderella. How well I remember so many of the incidents – Widow Twankey cooking in the kitchen and pulling out of an oven yards and yards of massive sausages, Cinderella sitting lonely by the fire and being greeted by her fairy godmother who proceeded to wave her wand and produce in the kitchen a stage coach and all the trimmings for Cinderella's new clothes, But the scene which really surpassed everything was the transformation scene at the end. This was a grand finale and the scenery of what seemed beautiful splendour was constantly changing as people walked to the front of the stage to receive their applause. Mother once told me some years later that Father had said that the look of amazement and pleasure on our faces when the curtain first went up more than repaid him for the cost of the day's outing.

~

Early in the 20th century, shortly after the end of the Boer War Baden Powell founded the Boy Scouts Movement. It quickly proved to be very popular and all my friends and I wished to join. I asked Father for permission to join but he refused. To his mind it was a military organization founded by an ex soldier. In spite of his refusal I, with some of my close friends, played at being scouts and performed their operations. We even found some fellow who was willing to become our scoutmaster but we never actually joined the organization.

On a later occasion a horse-race meeting was organized in Warrington. I wanted to see this spectacle but I was forbidden to go near the course. I did go and spent my time trying to peep under the canvas screen which had been put around the area. I did not see much. However when I got home rather late and was asked where I had been I had to confess to my disobedience. I was sent immediately to bed without anything to eat.

I was absolutely forbidden to read any 'bloods'* as we called them but I did read borrowed 'Sexton Blakes' on the sly. Father was quite fair about this because he bought plenty of good books for me to read and subscribed for a monthly children's magazine – *Chatterbox* – of which he approved.

Sometime in 1911 I sat for the Junior Oxford Local Examinations. In this examination two subjects were compulsory – English and Religious Knowledge. Religious Knowledge was not a subject which was taught in the Secondary School I attended. In fact I think it was forbidden under the Local Bye Laws. (Local authorities in England control education under the direction, guidance and grants of the Board of Education.) The Fathers of all the boys in my class who were taking the examination signed, without any hesitation, a form declaring that they objected to their sons taking this subject. Not so my Father. He refused to sign the form when I produced it. But as with several other of his prohibitions he found an alternative instead. He persuaded one of our friends to coach me in the specified subjects for the examination, namely Matthew and Samson I. It was Mr Elliott. He explained everything to me carefully and got me to write short essays on various aspects. In fact I expected to get a high distinction but I didn't.

I think Father gave me my first bicycle when I was eight and during the following years I explored every corner of Cheshire, generally with one or other of my friends. Occasionally on Sundays Father would take Ruth and me out for a ride. Another entertainment he provided for the family was to hire what was called a landau. It was a sort of miniature open coach in which three people could sit on each of two facing seats. I always sat with the driver of the horse and was sometimes allowed to hold the reins. I should say Father hired one of these vehicles nearly every summer. Mother used to enjoy these outings because it was the only way she got around the Cheshire countryside. I remember trips to Knutsford, Lymn, Delamere Forest, Frodsham and Acton Bridge. We usually took sweets and things to eat on the journey but we always pulled up at some hotel for lunch.

Father was not a teetotaler but he was only a modest and occasional drinker. I never saw him in any way affected but Mother once told me that in

* Editors: 'Bloods' were lightweight literature, which Walter's father thought not worth Walter's time. Sexton Blake was a fictional detective, somewhat like Sherlock Holmes.

the early months of their marriage he had come home in a condition which she had never seen before and never saw again. Her only comment was 'I wondered what I was in for'. Mother was a bit of a prude at the time when she told this story and even now I think she must have exaggerated a little. I remember four events in which his drinking, if such it could be called, played a part.

When I was about ten the family was taken to Blackpool for a holiday. One very hot afternoon when I was returning to our boarding-house after a walk with him, he suddenly stopped and said 'you go back now. I'm just going along here'. I knew what was down the other road. But he could not have had more than one drink because he was back in our rooms shortly after I arrived.

Another time we were spending the Christmas and New Year holidays at a Hydro, in Matlock, Derbyshire. On New Year's Eve, just after midnight, the waiters carried into the ballroom, where Father and I were standing, a large steaming bowl of hot punch. The waiters filled glasses with the punch and handed them round to the assembled guests. Father took one and so did I. I was about fourteen and had never had anything like this before but I was quite willing to give it a trial. My Father, after draining his glass, saw me wondering what to do. 'Here', he said, 'I'll take that' and he did.

We had a wonderful holiday at this Hydro. Matlock is at the southern end of the Pennine Range and is very hilly. We were there for about ten days and during this period the ground was covered with at least a foot of snow. The Hydro, provided a number of toboggans for the use of their guests. I got one and with Ruth and another girl tugged it up a steep road for at least a mile. It was all worth the effort for we had all the thrills in the world on the run down the road at high speed – at least my impression at the time was of high speed. Nevertheless it was certainly faster than I had ever gone down a steep hill on a bicycle.

I had better explain that Hydro, is short for Hydropathic Establishment, in other words a hotel where the guests can have treatment, by water, for various diseases. I do not recall what facilities for treatment existed in this place. If there were any they were not very prominent. But they did have a pump room where you could drink as much as you wanted of the mineral water pumped out of the ground. I only tried it once but it was too awful to try again.

I was much older on the third drinking occasion, about seventeen I should think. At that time Father kept a crate of Guinness in the cellar from which he had from time to time a glass for 'medicinal purposes'. Mr Elliott had called in and been invited to stay for supper. He was the person who, as I recounted earlier, coached me for my Religious Knowledge examination. He was one of the leading figures in the Baptist Chapel, deeply religious but a very fine man of whom the whole family was very fond. As we were sitting down to supper Father, much to my disgust, ordered me to fetch a bottle of Guinness from the cellar. I remember going down the cellar steps cursing my Father for putting on such a performance in front of a pillar of the Chapel who must, because of his Baptist beliefs, be a staunch teetotaler. After my Father had taken the stopper off the bottle he, in his most polite manner, asked Mr Elliott if he would like some. And to my absolute amazement he said he would. Still more of the facts of life were brought home to me at that moment.

Finally when, in 1948, Val (my wife) and I were on our first visit back to England from Australia we were driving around Yorkshire and stopped at some country pub for lunch. I asked Father if he would have a preliminary drink and he ordered a sherry. I had always been used to sipping sherry but Father tossed his off in one swift gulp. I was amazed at his performance. Afterwards it struck me that this must have been the 'done thing' among the young bloods in his youth.

~

My Father was a really talented 'cello player who loved his instrument which he continued to play until just before his death when he complained that his fingers were no longer supple. He had been taught in the first place by his great friend Nathan Crowther who was my Mother's brother. I have always believed, but never been told, that he fell in love with my Mother when she opened the door on his arrival for a lesson. Even the earlier part of the story is interesting. Uncle Nathan had himself been required to go to work in a woollen mill, like my mother. In the house there was still a 'cello which had been played by his father who died when my Mother was very young, and also by his father before him. Uncle Nathan came home one day and said to his Mother that he had decided to take lessons which he did and became a very competent artist. He became a teacher himself and in 1909 went to the United States to further his career. He had been promised a professional place in the Chicago Philharmonic Orchestra but someone let him down. He drifted from teaching into playing in a Cinema and then when the talkies came in he had to make his living by teaching again.

After he settled in Warrington, my Father went to Manchester once a week for lessons with a German or Austrian musician, well known at that time, Carl Fuchs, who was a Professor at the Manchester College of Music. His pupil must have shown talent, because in his time, my Father was the most renowned 'cello player for miles around Warrington. He did some teaching. He was the leader in a very good amateur orchestra and he was in constant demand to play solos at concerts. Every Sunday afternoon for many years there was a quartette in our house. On certain evenings he would be out at a friend's place playing more chamber music. I don't know whether this sort of thing goes on nowadays but it was before the days of television, or even of radio, when people had to provide their own entertainment.

Well! the result of all this enthusiasm for the cello was that he thought that I, who had been preceded, as I have recorded, by at least three generations of 'cello players must have some latent inborn talent for the instrument. He therefore, when I was eight years of age, bought a small size 'cello for me to play. Unfortunately he chose to teach me himself and with his irascibility it was a fatal decision. I had seven years of agony from his teaching. I don't think I have a genuine ear for music although over the years I did make some slight progress in my performing skill. But I was made to practice for at least an hour a day, which I hated, and my Mother kept a close watch on the time I put in. Towards the end I was capable of putting a book on the music stand and reading until my Mother called out about the horrible scratching noises I was making in playing scales automatically. But the real trouble began when my Father got me to himself for at least two hours on Sunday evening in the sitting room. It always ended in a row and frequently I was sent to bed in disgrace. The trouble was that he used to get cross when I did not perform as well or with such expression as he wanted. The more furious he became the more recalcitrant was I. In fact I used to deliberately play a note off tune to irritate him. So I have to admit that he had something 'up with', as Churchill would have said 'he would not put'.

The climax came when after some years of this misery he knocked the 'cello out of my hands, boxed my ears and ordered me off to bed. I got half way up the stairs, looked at him over the bannisters where he stood watching my departure, and then yelled out at him 'You villain' whereupon he came after me as fast as he could run. I bolted upstairs to the lavatory, tried to lock the door but he beat me to it and forced the door open. He demanded that I should promise never to speak with such insolence to him again. When I hesitated he boxed my ears again and continued to do so until he had extracted some sort of a promise from me. I don't think it was actually the end of my cello lessons because I am certain that the next day he was more repentant than I was. The lessons did, however, not continue for very much longer.

Walter (b. 1896) and his sister, Ruth (b. 1897). These early professional photographs of Walter and Ruth, dressed in their best, were taken in 1898 and 1906 respectively.

The second photo shows Walter holding a cello. The photo is printed to be a postcard. Although the card was not posted, Ruth has written on it and addressed it to their mother Mary at the family's Warrington address. Ruth's note reads:

> My Dear Mother,
> Do you know these children? I hope Dada had a nice holiday. I think uncle must have a sweet heart now. I am going to Auntie Tib's on Monday. [Illegible] hoping you are getting better.
> Ruth

~

My Father was the only person of his generation who, as far as I know, made any attempt to tell his son a few of the facts of life. I am certain that none of my friends had any instruction at all. I remember that he was a little shy and cautious at first, as I was when I tried to initiate my own sons. But I give him full credit for doing a good job. I had heard some of the fundamentals of the subject when I was extremely young, certainly by the age of eight, but I pretended to be ignorant when he started his explanation. But unlike so many boys I did not have any sex problems either at or after the age of puberty. In fact I don't remember that these matters were discussed at all after I started at the Secondary School. I may have heard, and even repeated, certain dirty stories based on the sex theme, but that was all. The only experience, indirectly related to the subject was a handling of my genitals by a tailor, employed by my Father. He fiddled around every time I tried on a new suit. I could not understand his action, was very much embarrassed by it, but did not know what to do. At last when I was about 17 I gave him a good shove while he was bending beside me and sent him rolling along the floor. About this time a friend of mine was treated in the same way by the same man and he was just as incensed as I was but he did nothing about it either. I did not tell my Father until many years later. He wished I had told him at the time. He said he had once had a complaint of the fitter's behaviour but could not believe it, so did nothing about it. As a matter of fact the fitter was a leading light in his church.

~

In his business my Father called himself a Tailor and Draper but he had never learnt anything about the practical side of tailoring. He owned and managed a very prosperous business which was really a time-payment enterprise. He and his brother, who later became his partner, and several men they employed, travelled around the neighbouring towns soliciting orders and collecting weekly payments on the outstanding amounts owed by poor people who, for the most part, lived in very lowly houses, but not in slums. He wanted me to join him in this business and first suggested I should do so when I was about 16. I had already set my eyes on the Civil Service but he said I would earn far more money with him than I would ever get as a Civil Servant. But I refused to consider the idea. For one thing I had developed a real loathing for the time payment business and I knew that with our clashing personalities I would not be happy in a business association with him. I never told him what my real objections were but said I wanted to try for the Civil Service.

I think I have said enough to illustrate the main features of my Father's character. I hope I have been fair to him. I never heard him complain of the life he had led or suggest that the fates had been unkind to him. He never suggested that he had been frustrated. All the same it is a pity he did not find better outlets for his talents. He was a very able and intelligent man and, unlike my mother, had received a grammar school education. He could have been successful in a more satisfying and stimulating job than the one in which he spent the greater part of his life.

Warrington – Pre-1914

I have jotted down a few more notes about life in Warrington during the first fourteen years of the 20th century. But before embarking on these I must recount a little of the history of Warrington. It is without doubt, one of the oldest towns in the County of Lancashire and its motto which appears on the Borough Coat of Arms, *Deus dat incrementum** also appeared on my prefect's badge when I was at the Secondary School. Due to its geographical position on the River Mersey, Warrington was of significance to the early Britons long before the Roman invasion of Britain. Axes dating from the Bronze Age have been found in the district. The Romans maintained a ford across the river and a station on the site where Warrington stands was called 'Veratinum'. There was a Saxon fort nearby and the place was occupied by the Danes. It gets a mention in Domesday Book. The town was visited by successive kings right up to the time of George VI but the one of particular interest is recorded at Thelwall, a nearby hamlet, where my parents lived from 1928 onwards. Its 'Pickering Arms' has long borne a sign reading 'In 923 Edward the Elder founded a city here and called it Thelwall'.

Throughout its history Warrington has been a market place for the rural activities of the district. Its early manufacturing industries catered for these activities but after the Industrial Revolution it concentrated mainly on chemicals and the manufacture of wire. The local professional Rugby team was always called the 'wire pullers'. A wire puller, or more correctly a 'wire drawer', was a worker who pulled the red hot wire through appropriate gauges

---

* Editors: God giveth the increase.

to reduce it to the required diameter. When I was a boy it used to be terribly hard work for the workers but nowadays they tell me it is all powered by electricity and that computers direct the temperature of the wire, the speed at which it passes through the gauges, the size of the gauges, the length of wire drawn and I have no doubt other appropriate technical requirements.

The Manchester Ship Canal passes just outside Warrington. It was a great source of attraction for boys and according to one of my early school masters it had the same appeal for him and others during the days of its construction. I can think of four swing bridges and two high cantilever bridges which crossed the canal. The former were roadways on steel bridges which were swung to one side of the canal whenever a ship was approaching. The mechanism of cogged wheels and other devices under the bridge were fascinating to watch when the bridge was swinging round. The first time I was taken under a bridge to watch it swing I was scared and ran for my life. But the greatest attraction of all was the locks in which ocean liners were brought to a lower level of water if they were proceeding from Manchester to Liverpool and thence across the world.

I remember the steam rollers that used to move around the town. They had a huge cylinder as a wheel in front to crush anything in the way, usually road making material. There were also steam traction engines that pulled wagons. Both these contraptions travelled at less

Walter's son Peter in 1935, taking a photo of a ship seeming to steam through the fields, but really, steaming along the Manchester Ship Canal.

than five miles an hour but the law required that a man waving a red flag should walk in front of them. I suppose they were considered to be some source of danger to pedestrians and other vehicles but at the speed they travelled anybody could get out of the way. I believe a red flag used to be carried in front of the early motor cars, but I never saw that happening. The cars certainly did not travel at any great speed and it was just as well because the roads were not built to carry fast traffic. Most of the streets in Warrington were paved with cobble stones. The surrounding country roads were called Macadam after the inventor, and were made of a mixture of cement, sand and stones all pressed together until they became hard. I suppose that is where the steam rollers came into their own. In winter these roads were terribly muddy, and in summer very dusty. Motor cars used to stir up clouds of dust as they travelled along. That is why ladies always put up their sunshades or umbrellas if they saw a motor car approaching.

I must place on record a dear old soul named Miss Buckle. Father called her 'Buckle' and she liked it. I called her Auntie Buckle and she liked that too. When she was much younger she had worked as a seamstress for my Father's Uncle Alfred and then after my father acquired his Uncle's business, for him. She gave this up before I was born and moved to a house in which she took good class boarders. But she was always in financial trouble. She had no idea of controlling her expenses and wasted and gave away what bit of money she had. She always let bills mount up and every few years my Father had to clear her of debt. She was very fond of boys but never showed much interest in girls. I was her favourite boy. Until I was about eight she lived in a house next door but one to ours. I was in and out of her place two or three times every day. She always welcomed me. One day I went in and she was not there. In wandering around I accidentally knocked over a pot of ink on a small side table. The result was that the ink flowed all over a small red cloth lying over the table. I immediately turned the cloth upside down and, presumably because the ink had not soaked through, there was no damage to be seen. Later in the day when I was playing she came in to talk to my Mother. After a little while she said 'Someone came into my house this morning and knocked my inkpot over'.

I think I realized that she was letting me know that she knew who had done it. But I kept quiet and never confessed.

For years after this she was my mainstay whenever I got dirty boots. The grounds on which we played were often dirty but even more dirty were the ponds. I used to get into terrible trouble if I ever went home with dirty boots. My parents seemed to regard it as a sign that I had been doing something I shouldn't do. So for years I called in Auntie Buckle's before going home, to clean my shoes and if necessary my clothing. She was always willing to help me to keep out of trouble and always carefully inspected me, sometimes brushed my hair, before I returned home.

We had two theatres and a hippodrome in Warrington. One theatre was a very old place and I was never taken there. It was considered not quite respectable. It was known as the 'blood tub' because, I was told, whenever anybody was stabbed in a melodrama, some contrivance spurted out what appeared to be blood. The other theatre was quite respectable. I was taken by my parents, or by my school teachers, to all the Shakespeare's plays that F.R. Benson's company put on. Throughout the year the programmes were changed every week as different companies arrived in the town. The incoming plays were always advertised and I can remember the names of some that came every year. I recall particularly a play called 'Sunday'. Every year the town was plastered with signs saying 'Sunday comes on Monday, next week'. Another title that sticks in my mind was 'A victim of the Mormons'. As a matter of fact a party of evangelical Mormons used to visit the town every year. The word soon went round that they had arrived. Such terrible stories used to be told about them that people, and especially children, were scared. But we never heard that they had done anything wrong in Warrington. Nor could we have done because they were quite a respectable body. The Hippodrome was hardly a place for children but Father took us once to see Chung Ling Soo. He was quite a well known conjuror but was in fact an Englishman dressed as a Chinese. In our presence he performed his famous trick of apparently catching on a plate a bullet fired by an assistant. A bullet made a rattling noise on the plate after the report of the gun. Actually he was killed in this act a few years later.

The cinema really got going during my childhood. At first a travelling show used to come about once a year. Then they began to build new places or convert old halls into cinemas. One place even served afternoon tea at the matinees to the patrons in the best seats. One cinema had an open door at the front and you could see the operator standing in a box and turning the handle of the projector. The quality of the entertainment was measured by the number of pictures they showed. They sometimes advertised that 20 pictures were on offer. But of course they were all very short, lasting between 5 and 10 minutes.

I remember one evening, while I was kneeling at my Mother's knees saying my prayers, all the sirens in the town started a blasting noise. I can still hear Mother's voice saying 'Mafeking's relieved'. This was a town which had been under siege for 217 days during the Boer War. I think I was about four at this time but I knew enough to realize that people had been worried about the prolonged siege and so I understood Mother's remark. I remember watching, in 1910, Halley's Comet passing overhead. The most impressive part of the spectacle was the tail which appeared as a luminous glow trailing behind the comet. I say 'trailing' because that was the impression I got even though the comet was not apparently moving. In fact I have since learnt that owing to the attraction of the sun the tail always points towards the sun. The comet is due again in nine years time (1985) and I would like to be one of the few people to have seen it twice.*

In my very young days public transport consisted of horse-drawn buses. It used to be great fun to amble along in these slow moving vehicles with a complete view of everything around you. They were eventually replaced by open-topped trams. There was great excitement when on their first day of operation several illuminated trams traversed the route. I was taken out at night to see them. I really believe, though, that once we had got used to electric trams, we thought the old horse buses were more exciting.

Another incident relates to a holiday which the family had at Llandudno, on the north coast of Wales. I should first explain that Ruth, my sister, and I had both had, for some time, season tickets at the local baths. But we had

---

* Editors: Walter died in 1979.

never been together in the water. Sea bathing was available at Llandudno but we had never tried that. There were two adjoining areas, one for males and one for females. In order to bathe you entered a horse drawn caravan on wheels which was then pulled out into about two feet of water. Ruth and I agreed to meet at the line of subdivision between the areas for the two sexes. We did meet. I have nothing more to say about the meeting because the only point of the story is to indicate the sort of conditions under which sea-bathing was conducted in those days.

Finally before I go on to recall my schooldays I would like to tell something of the slums in Warrington and the people who lived in them. Here in Melbourne, we have recently had a report about the poverty in the city. The investigators were appalled at what they found. It is nothing compared with the conditions in Warrington at the beginning of the 20th century. In large areas of the town were masses of filthy old houses occupied by filthy people who went around in filthy rags. The men were usually unemployed and I don't know how they managed to pay for whatever food they obtained. A lot of them managed to get rolling drunk and were often carried off to the Police Station on a handcart. I don't remember hearing of any enquiry into conditions in the town and I don't know what charitable organizations existed. There was no need for an enquiry into conditions in Warrington, because we all knew about them – they were so obvious. People were inclined to blame drink or laziness for the conditions. I think they were due to ignorance more than anything else. These poor people were always in trouble but they had not the slightest idea how to tackle their problems. They just drifted along and accepted drifting as a way of life.

School

All the schools I attended, infants, primary and secondary were co-educational or as they were more commonly called in those days, mixed. I can recall only one person, Madge Knowles, who was in the same class with me from the beginning to the end.

I went to the infants' school when I had turned six and Ruth, who was 16 months younger was taken along with me. Father had already taught me to read. A Miss Bullen was the headmistress and she insisted on calling me 'Alfy' because she had previously had a pupil of that name, also a Balmford and a cousin of my Father's. I need only record one other recollection. We used to do all our writing on slates provided by the school. We had to take our own slate pencils. The slates were plain on one side. The other side was permanently marked by double lines. All down this side of the slate, there were sets of these double lines. Each set was about an inch apart. We had to write between these narrow parallel lines. The day used to start with the teacher shouting out 'Give out slates'. The monitors used to rush out, gather up a pile of slates and hand them to the other children. When we had finished with slates the teacher used to call out 'Hold up slates' whereupon we all held our slates in front of us shoulder high. She would then go along the rows of desks carrying a can of water and with a damp mop give each slate a dab. When she had got back to the front of the class she would call out 'Clean slates'. We all took pieces of cloth to school and with these we proceeded to remove all the markings from the slates. It all sounds very military but we used to enjoy it.

The primary school to which I went was in the street where we lived. It was an old nonconformist school called 'People's College' until it was taken over by the Borough Council. Although we were forbidden to call it by its old name we usually did. It was undoubtedly the best primary school in the town and was unusual in that fees were charged. The fees started at one penny a week in Standard I, thereafter increasing by one penny for each advancement until they became 6d. per week in Standard VI. I don't know what they were in VII because I left at the end of VI to go to the secondary school.

Many of the boys who lived some distance away used to get to school early in order to play beforehand. As we lived nearby, I usually got there just before the gate was shut. When the assembly was completed and the gate was opened the late boys were paraded before the headmaster and caned, if they were frequent offenders. When the school bell rang we all assembled in lines near to our class rooms. The headmaster, standing in the centre of all the boys (the girls were with the headmistress in their playground) called out 'Stand out those boys with dirty boots'. The masters then went along the lines of boys to see if the offenders had revealed themselves. The defaulters were then marched off for similar punishment. In fairness I must admit that this procedure was not carried out on wet days when most shoes would be soiled.

All that I remember of Standard I is that the mistress, Miss Wolmersley, used to have a really difficult time trying to teach the children that a noun was only the name of an object. Many of them found it difficult to distinguish between the name and the object itself. I was in Standard I in 1903. Forty four years later in 1947, when I was in Australia, my sister Olive wrote to tell me that Miss Wolmersley was in Adelaide. So I arranged by letter to meet her outside the Post Office there on my next visit. Believe it or not we recognised one another after that long interval. I had not seen her since 1903 because she left Warrington at the end of that year. I took her to some place for afternoon tea and we found quite a lot to talk about. She then took me to meet her brother who was an entomologist at a city museum. He was older than I and although I had never really known him, I had often seen him departing with his father, both burdened with butterfly nets and other gear to go on a day's expedition in the country. So a hobby became his life work.

Standard III saw the beginning of my interest in mathematics. The mistress asked the class this question, 'If a bottle and a cork cost 1½d'. and the bottle costs a penny more than the cork, what does the cork cost?' She went around the class and asked every child in turn for the answer. They all said '½d'. She then said 'only one boy has got the right answer', and it was I. She then tested me out on different amounts but I had already worked out how to do the calculation. The other matter relates to Ruth who, in the termly grade promotion was moved up every time, while I remained stationary in Standard 3(a). Each standard was divided into three sections (a), (b) and (c) of which (a) was the top. So I had watched her climb up from 2(a) to 3(b) in trepidation and to my horror at the beginning of the third term she was brought up to my standard 3(a). There may be an explanation of my shortcomings revealed in the opening remarks about Standard IV which follow.

There is no doubt that until I got into Standard IV, I had been completely bored during the whole of my three years at school. I know this was because I was not stretched at all. For instance, as soon as we were handed new readers I, while keeping my eye on the place where the hesitating child was trying to read aloud, had read the whole of the stories in the book in no time. Hence I had nothing to do but daydream. But the freeze (for such it was) broke when I went into Standard IV, and for the first time I had a teacher who could really create an interest for us. Mr Knowles was his name and I record it with pleasure and admiration for him. I don't know what they called the subject in those days (in fact I think it was one of his own invention) but today it would be 'current affairs'. In 1906, the year in which I entered Standard IV, the newly elected Liberal Government in Britain advocated a policy of complete trust of the Boers, who had been defeated in the War two years earlier, and forthwith instituted self-government in the newly established colonies. I don't know whether I would ever have learnt anything about this episode from other sources if Mr Knowles had not explained the story about South Africa to us. The whole emphasis at the time was on the magnanimity of the British offer to the South Africans so soon after their defeat. But I have no doubt that it was also considered to be in the best interests of Britain as well. Mr Knowles secured pictures of various incidents in the handing over of responsibility, which were pasted on the Notice Board. We had lectures from him on Shakespeare's plays. As it happened we had been reading some plays aloud at home with Father so I was aware of the names of most of the plays. I was one of the few children in the class to call out names of the plays when Mr Knowles asked us to do so. At this time we had a boy in the class whose name was Leah. This boy came from a very poor home and even in winter was without shoes and stockings – not an uncommon sight in those days. When I called out 'King Lear' this boy turned round, looked at me in amazement and when he realized that he had heard me correctly he stood up, threw back his head and shoulders and thumping his chest with pride called out 'King Lear, King Lear, That's me'. I could go on telling of many things in which Mr Knowles aroused my interest. But I will tell just one of how I got his interest in something. One of the rules of grammar which he struggled hard to drive into our heads was that 'a preposition governs a noun in the objective case'. One day when a girl (I even remember her name) made the usual mistake when parsing aloud a short sentence he called out in despair 'For the forty thousandth time I have told you that a preposition does so and so'. The very next person made exactly the same mistake when parsing another sentence. This was too much for Mr Knowles and he made the same anguished cry as before. I do not know how I had the courage to do so but I immediately called out 'Forty thousand and first, Sir'. He looked at me and grinned. Thereafter whenever the same mistake was made again he turned to me and said 'What's the number this time, Balmford?' I counted up two, three, etc. and always knew the appropriate number when he made the call. This joke really taught the class to remember the rule.

I had diphtheria towards the end of the school holidays in summer 1907 so I was three weeks late in joining the class in Standard V. When I got home I told my Father that during my absence the class had been learning something called 'Algebra' and that it involved adding a's and b's together which I could not understand. The next day he came home with Hall and Stevens Elementary Algebra. From then on he, Uncle Jimmy and I had, every Sunday evening, what I thought was a wonderful game, learning all the various tricks in algebra. I soon outclassed my seniors and of course by the end of the school year we had finished the book and were miles ahead of the class. This was the second stage in the development of my interest in mathematics.

My crowning glory came in Standard VI when the master got stuck on the board in the solution of a problem in algebra. He had discovered that I had acquired some skill in the subject, so he turned to me and asked how I had solved the problem. I had had a bit of trouble myself in forming an equation which was soluble by methods known to me. In seeking an alternative approach I lit on the idea that the trick was to let 'x' equal something other than the more obvious unknown. This had enabled me to solve the problem. This master and I got on very well but he often pulled my leg. For instance, the class was taking it in turn, to parse the words in a list of sentences in our grammar book. I noticed that he was, from time to time, passing over certain boys but it afterwards became evident that he was planning to make me do a certain sentence. When it came to my turn I first read out the sentence. I had to parse. It was 'My hair had known no comb since I left London'. He immediately said 'I should not think it had either'. I expect it was his annual joke when a class did those sentences.

And that was the end of my time at the Primary School. I had taken the Entrance Examination for the Secondary School and came, I think, 8th out of the 60 who were successful. I was to transfer to the new School in September 1909.

~

The Warrington Secondary School, where I was to stay for five years, was provided with a new and very modern building. Secondary Education in England, as compared with that of several European countries, had been neglected until 1902. The Education Act of that year provided for the establishment of new secondary schools under the control of Local Authorities but supervised and largely financed by the Board of Education. Warrington was one of the first towns to take action under this Act. When I first went there the first batch of students who entered into the new school in 1903 had just left. The school was very well equipped, especially in the physics, chemistry, woodwork and biology laboratories and a good staff of teachers had been recruited. If there was one fault it was that the nucleus of the school had been created out of an institution which prepared people for entry into a Teachers' Training College. As a result too much of the curriculum in the higher forms continued to be directed to this same objective. Harold Emmerson and I were the first people to sit for the Second Division Civil Service Examination. Previously boys, at age 16, had sat for the minor Boy Clerks Examination which was a disgrace because the successful candidates entered a blind alley. The curriculum of the top form in the school was not adjusted in the slightest to meet the needs of those taking the Second Division examination or the Matriculation. Consequently we had to do a lot of private study both at home and in school, with some, but not much, supervision in order to master some of the subjects in both examinations.

On entering the Secondary School I was placed in Form 2 and then on to Forms 4, 5, 6 and Bursars. I won a scholarship in Form 4 for free books and tuition which was renewed every year with a cash grant of £10 per annum. When I went to the Borough Treasurer to collect my cash I was paid in ten gold sovereigns.

I was never a good sportsman at school. If I could get out of cricket or football which were more or less compulsory, I could always find something much better to do. The only sport in which I distinguished myself was swimming. I did play football for the House eleven but they never risked putting me in the school First Eleven. I was a little more interested in cricket and was chosen to play for the First Eleven in the first match of the 1914 season because so very few people had returned to school from the 1913 team. In this match I made a magnificent catch by running backwards to keep my eye on a very high ball and, by some stroke of good luck, the ball stayed in my hands. As a result I played for the whole season. I usually went in first because nobody liked being an opener. I don't think I ever made more than ten runs but as a spin bowler I took, a few wickets.

During the first year at school I was introduced to French and Science for the first time. In Form 4 I was top in French for the only occasion. I don't know why but even at the time I suspected the mistress must have added up my marks incorrectly. In Form 4 I was helped by a good master to develop further interest in mathematics. This was encouraged still further in Form 5 by an even more wonderful master who was the new Deputy Head. I remember that in that form everybody was confused by the multiplicity of names for stock and share prices i.e. nominal value, issue price, market price, bonus price, maturity price, etc. etc. When Mr Broome realized this he formed first a company and then a Stock Exchange. Various students had different roles in each of these bodies. I think I was an Auditor. But the company went through the process of raising capital and then issuing shares. We all then started buying shares on the stock exchange and these transactions were put through by people who had been made brokers. It was an excellent idea. I certainly learnt what the subject 'Stocks and Shares' in Arithmetic was all about.

In 1912 my Father and Mother went to America to visit Mother's brother, Nathan Crowther, in Chicago. I don't know whether they were considering settling there. While they were away I stayed with Uncle Jimmie who was Father's business partner. I had just taken the Oxford Local Examinations which I referred to earlier in connection with Mr Elliott. In the examination syllabus I had noticed a mathematical subject, 'Calculus', which I had never heard of before. I therefore went to the Local Library and borrowed a book on the subject. I spent a good part of my summer holidays working through the whole of this text-book and working out many of the examples. This was another stage in my mathematical development.

Early photo of Walter as a young man, about 1912.

By the time I had reached Form 6 it had been agreed that I should sit for the Second Division Civil Service Examination. I proceeded to work for it and as I said earlier most of the work was by private study. When the results of the examination came out in November 1913 Harold Emmerson and I were in the second part of the printed results – i.e. unsuccessful candidates. But he was only a little way after the last of the 100 successful candidates. On 5th August 1914, the day after War was declared, he got a telegram telling him to report to the Admiralty. I was too far down the unsuccessful list ever to be offered an appointment. So I had to start work again for the next examination in September 1914. Harold Emmerson thought he had missed an appointment at this time so we started swotting together. He helped me a lot and gave me coaching in 'Mechanics' at his home. As a result of his delayed appointment it was only I who had to sit for the examination in September 1914. I got the same treatment as Harold. There were again 100 successful candidates out of over 2000 and I think I was about 110th. So the report on the results was accompanied by a letter telling me, after a medical examination, to report at once to the War Office.

Walter, seated, with Billy Williams, St James's Park, London, 1916.
Photo taken by Harold Emmerson.

Just prior to my sitting for the Civil Service examination for the second time in September 1914 the First World War broke out. When this happened Ruth and I were staying with Uncle Sanderson, Father's eldest brother at Longwood near Huddersfield in the house where my Father was born. There was some bewilderment when War was declared and I don't think people generally understood what would be involved. Ruth and I returned home the following day. We had to change trains at Manchester and I well remember the crowds of soldiers on the station platforms. They were probably reservists who had been recalled to the colours.

A few days after my return to Warrington an appeal was issued by Lord Kitchener for men over age 18 to enlist in what was eventually to be called 'Kitchener's Army'. As Warrington was the headquarters of the South Lancashire Regiment there were barracks in the town. These became the recruiting centre and I spent a whole day with a friend, Willie Healey, trying to enlist. The barracks were packed with volunteers and we were unable to get anywhere near the Recruiting Officer. When I got back home I was asked where I had been all day. On confessing that I had been trying to enlist my Mother made a remark which I will never forget. 'Why did you do that? You know very well that we pay men to fight for us'. Today that seems a very cold-hearted and nasty remark but it should be read in the context of the times. In the first place my Mother had not realized that the country would be compelled to raise a large voluntary army. But I think she was more influenced by her knowledge of the soldiers who were garrisoned in the Warrington barracks. It may be a hard thing to say but they were mostly the scum of the unemployed. Moreover when they were decked up in their red-coats they were a great attraction to many of the girls especially servant girls with often dire consequences. My Mother had tried hard to protect servant girls who had lived in our house but I recall that at least one had to leave because of advanced pregnancy. So it can be well understood that my Mother had no wish for me to consort with such people.

London – 1914–17

As I indicated earlier the First World War had already broken out when on 17th December 1914, I left Warrington for London to take up my appointment at the War Office. I had no idea how to get to Margravine Gardens, Barons Court when the train arrived at Euston so, for the first time in my life, I hired a taxi. This address was where Harold Emmerson was boarding. It was run by Mrs McPhee and her married daughter Mrs Dyer. Mr Dyer who was a Sergeant in a Territorial Regiment, the Post Office Rifles, had been called up in August 1914 and was already serving in France. I suppose I must have written to say that I was coming because there was a bed alongside Harold's waiting for me on arrival. Harold, who was working late every night at the Admiralty did not arrive back in the digs (as we called them) until after about nine o'clock. I remember him giving a yell on entering the house because he recognized something of mine in the hall.

The next day I reported to the War Office in Whitehall and was taken to what was called Accounts 3. This was one of many branches administered by the Financial Secretary of the War Office. It dealt with the payment of Separation Allowances to the families of serving soldiers. Most of the detailed work was done in the Army Pay Offices throughout the United Kingdom, but because of the complications which arose when parents had more than one son in the Army such cases were handled in the Section where I served. There were many females employed in this Branch, one of which was a very attractive girl named Florence Valantine. I married her eight years later. I would say there was only one female typist in our branch and most of the letters which had to be typed were done by boy-clerks, a corps of very juvenile temporary clerks. Very important letters were always typed on thick tinted paper and concluded with the words 'I am, Sir, Your very obedient Servant'. I did not sign such letters. The ones I signed were mostly enquiries. I wrote my questions on the left-hand side of a sheet of paper with a printed letter head and opening printed words such as 'I am directed by the Assistant Financial Secretary of the War Office to enquire'. A reply paid envelope was enclosed and the person was expected to return the sheet with his answers on the right hand side of the paper.

Walter – Man of Peace. War Office 1915, in the National Portrait Gallery, Trafalgar Square, London, which was taken over by the War Office for the duration. Walter and his future wife, Val, met while they were both working in the Gallery.

There was another Warrington fellow living in the house – Freddy Hughes. He had been in the office of Crosfield's Soap Works in Warrington and had been sent to assist in the firm's London office. After a few months he enlisted in the Westminster Rifles and there joined Ben Farrar, an old school friend, who had been attending but had not completed a two-year's course

Walter and Val on their wedding day, 22 June 1922 at St Luke's Church, West Norwood, London.

at Westminster Training College. Freddy was killed in the Somme battle of 1916. Ben, although wounded, survived the War and eventually returned to Westminster College in 1919.

While I was living in London at this time and also when I returned after the War, my Father's youngest brother (Joseph William) and Auntie Lizzie were always very kind to me. He was a Civil Servant in the Exchequer and Audit Department. They welcomed me round to their house at Chiswick at the week-end whenever I wanted to go.

Of course, when I first arrived in London, I was anxious to see as much of the place as possible. I often bought a bar of chocolate for lunch and visited all the famous buildings in Westminster. At the week-ends I explored the city and such places as Hyde Park, Kensington Gardens, Hampstead Heath, Barnes Common, Richmond Park and Hampton Court Palace. I very soon learnt my way around London and especially the best routes by bus, tram or tube, on which to get to places. Even today the buses on many routes bear the same numbers they did 60 years ago and even more remarkable I remember many of them.

After Harold and I had settled in London we went to the theatres (and especially the Old Vic) fairly frequently. It cost 4d. to sit in the pit in this particular theatre. It was built in 1818 and was named the Old Vic in 1886 when it became Trust property. Emma Cons and her niece, Lilian Baylis, became Joint Managers in 1898. Thereafter mainly Shakespeare's and Restoration plays were produced. Ben Greet was the manager when I started to go there and throughout most of the War Sybil Thorndyke and her husband Lewis Casson were the principal actors. The production of these plays and the quality of the actors were superb even though the scenery was often a little primitive. During the first two years in London I must have seen, at least once, twenty Shakespearean plays and four or five Restoration plays.

By the end of 1915 recruitment for the Army was declining but the insistent demand for men remained. Employment in the War Office was regarded as a reserved occupation so in spite of numerous attempts I was not allowed to enlist. In 1915 Lord Derby introduced what was called the 'Derby Scheme'. People who enlisted under this arrangement were promised that they would not be called up immediately and that single men would be called before married men. I enlisted under this scheme on 6th December 1915 but the War Office would not let me go. It was really a bit of a swindle because single men were called up very quickly and the married men shortly afterwards.

In 1916 Harold and I left our digs in Baron's Court and went to live in Carlingford Road, Hampstead. I don't remember for certain why we left our old place but I think we had got tired of the quality of the food. We did not stay in Carlingford Road very long because the landlady, Mrs Brown with a husband in the Army and a newly arrived baby, could no longer run the place. So we moved to South Hill Park Gardens, in which our house had a rear view of the Hampstead Ponds. It was summer and I used to go for a swim every morning before breakfast. Harold was no swimmer, so I went alone. We did not stay here very long because the landlady, Mrs Atwell, was such 'a so and so'. She was a mean sour faced woman.

She would not let us have a decent light or any heat in our private sitting room. Harold recently recalled coming home one night and finding me huddled up in my overcoat and seated on an armchair which I had lifted on to the table so as to be near the light. We left here fairly quickly and moved to Plympton Road, Brondesbury. I did not stay here very long because in February 1917 I was allowed by the War Office to join the Army. Both Harold and I returned to these lodgings after the War and I give a description of them in the chapter headed London 1919–38.

Royal Flying Corps – 1917–18

After having received from the War Office the necessary permission to enlist I applied for admission to the Artists Rifles. I was interviewed by a board of officers and accepted. In February 1917 I was called to the Regimental Headquarters near those Squares in Bloomsbury where I, along with other recruits, were given our uniforms and for several days were drilled in the gardens in the centre of one of the Squares. During this period I lived with Uncle Joseph and Auntie Lizzie at Chiswick. The Artists Rifles was a London Regiment in the Territorial Army. At the beginning of the War it had been designated an Officers' Training Corps but throughout the War it maintained its 'E' company at Montreul in France on guard duty at General Headquarters. There were at least three other Companies 'A', 'B' and 'C' (I don't remember a 'D') and these were stationed at Romford in Essex. Over the years the regiment had developed certain traditions, some of which were a little peculiar. For instance all sportsmen were in 'A' company while the Musicians and Artists were allocated to 'B' company, and the Writers were in 'C' company. The most peculiar assignment of all was of barristers and solicitors to the Cook-House. Training in law was the sole qualification. After over two years of war these various classifications had largely lost their significance but the cook house qualification had been fairly well maintained largely, I suppose, because the men involved were older. Well those are the conditions I learnt about when, after a week's training in London, we were sent down to a camp at Romford in Essex where we lived in huts. I don't remember any reason why I should have been posted to 'B' company.

Our officers were rather elderly, unfit for active service, and with few exceptions had served in the ranks of the Artists Rifles before the war. We had a few specialists from the Regular Army and our Colonel was an old retired Indian Army Officer

The training throughout the three months I was at Romford was very intensive. We performed daily the regular squad drill, sometimes company drill and I think battalion drill on one occasion Other activities included route marches, bayonet fighting, musketry and shooting practice at Purfleet on the Thames, fatigues, guard duty and physical training. I was only on guard duty once but I recall very clearly being out on the job on a very dark night. About midnight the sergeant of the guard, an old Regular Army man, came round on an inspection. He asked me when I would use my sentry box, to which I replied 'during inclement weather'. He then said 'What do you mean, when it's wet?' Whenever the physical training instructor was himself getting a bit tired, and we were very tired, he used to point to a lonely tree about half-a-mile away and call out 'Round that tree and back at the double. Go!' The most objectionable fatigue I had was in the hospital where I had to clean out the lavatories which had been fouled by patients with chronic diarrhoea. The best fatigue was in the officers' mess where, after serving at dinner at night, we were given a good meal and if we wanted but I did not, all the drinks available.

As a matter of fact I was often hungry in this camp at night. I suppose it was all the exercise and fresh air. Quite often I had to go to the Church Army Hut at about nine o'clock. Here you could get a good hot meal. There was also a Salvation Army Hut. I got caught in there once with Willie Schofield and another chap. The Chaplain enticed us into his room to run a prayer meeting. When the other three had said their pieces they waited in vain for me to follow suit.

The Commanding Officer, a fiery old Indian Army Colonel used to give a lecture to each batch of new recruits soon after they arrived. The title of the lecture was 'How to behave as a gentleman'. It was indeed quite good and was intended to help us if and when we were granted commissions. In one part of the lecture he talked about swearing and as I remember exactly what he said I will repeat his words which were 'I don't mind a 'bugger' or a 'damn', I don't mind a 'bloody' but there are two little words, one beginning with 'f' and another with 'c' which no gentleman uses'.

About three months after my arrival at Romford a general invitation was sent out for people to join the 'Royal Flying Corps'. It appealed to me because it seemed that your life in the Flying Corps depended more on your own skill and resourcefulness than it did if you were stuck in the trenches with the Infantry. So I applied to join and was duly interviewed by our Company Commander, Captain Rust. He seemed very impressed because I had printed my particulars on the application card I had to complete. The end result was that he recommended my transfer to the Royal Flying Corps. The Corps was part of the Army. The Royal Air Force was not created until April 1918.

~

In May 1917 I left the Artists Rifles and went to a Flying Corps Cadet School at Reading in Berkshire. We lived in the students residential college, Wantage Hall, at Reading University College. We were extremely comfortable and well fed there. We stayed in the hostel for three weeks until we moved into tents for one week. We continued to wear the same uniforms except that we were given Flying Corps 'split arse' caps. These were triangular shaped caps which were worn on the right-hand side of the head. The bottom of the caps were ringed by a white strip to indicate that we were cadets. The course which we took was well managed and the classes were conducted by capable lecturers. At the close of each morning session we learnt the morse code and practised, both receiving and sending on a buzzer. The rest of the day was spent on the theory of flight, rigging, engines, a few vague theories on aerial combat and machine guns. We had to be able to dismantle and reassemble Vickers and Lewis machine guns quickly and efficiently. The lecturers were mostly technical sergeants and I remember one sergeant in particular, who amused us by constantly repeating during his lecture 'I myself personally'. In fact we called him that.

I acquired a very good elementary knowledge of the Theory of Flight which he taught, and which was very useful to me in France when I was caught in a nasty situation. At the end of a month at Reading we were to proceed to a Flying School. There were a number of these schools all over the country and in a book, in the Adjutant's Office at Reading, we could enter in order of choice the names of the schools where we would like to be trained. It was understood that the choices, would be allocated in order of merit on the results of the examination we were to take at the end of the course. I know my first choice was Acton because it was close to London. I think that place was nearly everybody's first choice. I was one of the few people who did any studying for that examination and I was one of three people who were delighted to find themselves posted to Acton when the results of the examination appeared on a Notice Board. At this stage we were granted our commissions and a tailor came to measure us for our uniforms. The R.F.C. tunics were what we called 'maternity jackets' because the front was one broad piece of cloth instead of having buttons down the centre. The uniforms were ready in no-time and then, all dressed up, the three of us set off for Acton. I well remember that on the way to the railway station one of the other two chaps started to salute an oncoming officer and pulled up when he realized his mistake. The officer was amused and guessed we were newly fledged.

~

When I arrived at Acton I found that we were to live in tents (two officers in each tent) at the side of an aerodrome. The messing was contracted for by a civilian and his son. Neither the manager nor his son were very prepossessing and I regret to say that many of the chaps treated them in a very discourteous manner; the son was always called 'Lightning' for the speed with which he did not serve us. It was a bit of an ordeal going into an officers' mess for the first time for dinner, but it was just the same as anywhere else. At breakfast the next morning one of the chaps unscrewed the top off a salt cellar because it would not pour properly. In my innocence I thought 'Fancy doing that in an officers' mess'.

Army Form B. 2079.

WARNING.—*If you lose this Certificate a duplicate cannot be issued.*

Certificate of discharge of No. 765154 (Rank) Pte

(Name) Raleinford, Walter Crowther

(Regiment) 2/28th London Regt

who was enlisted at Fulham

on the 6th December 1915.

He is discharged in consequence of being appointed to Commission, Royal Flying Corps

after serving - years 112 days with the Colours, and 1 years 53 days in the Army Reserve.

(Place) London

(Date) 19/5/14

Signature of Commanding Officer: C.P. Stew. MAJOR FOR

*Description of the above-named man on 19 5 14. when he left the Colours.

Age 20 7/12

Height 5-4

Complexion

Eyes

Hair

Marks or Scars, whether on face or other parts of body.

**Should agree with the description on Character Certificate, Army Form B. 2067*

(A7715) Wt. W16563/M1858 200,000 3/17 D.D. & L. Sch. 44. Forms/B 2079/21

N.B.—Any person finding this Certificate is requested to forward it, in an unstamped envelope, to the Secretary, War Office, London, S.W.

Walter's Certificate of Discharge, when he transferred from the Artists Rifles after one year and 53 days in the Army Reserve, dated 19 May 1914. The discharge was required for him to transfer to the Royal Flying Corps, which was still part of the Army. The Royal Air Force was not formed until 1918.

Walter in the uniform of the Royal Flying Corps in 1918. Joining the Royal Flying Corps appealed to Walter because 'it seemed that your life in the Flying Corps depended more on your own skill and resourcefulness than it did if you were stuck in the trenches with the Infantry'.

The instructors were French civilians who taught us to fly on French Caudrons. I heard that the school was paid £100 for each pupil. These Frenchmen were not very good; their accent, especially in the air with a noisy engine was difficult to follow. Moreover they never explained anything properly. For instance on the first occasion when I had taken over control (sitting in front of the instructor) he yelled out 'Pull zee bloodee steek back' (steek was his pronunciation of stick). I was a bit slow in pulling back the stick because I could feel a resistance to any movement and thought the instructor must be imposing this restriction as a safeguard. I was used to the stick being floppy and easy to move on the ground. I now realized that the resistance was due, when in flight, to the air pressure on the elevator. We practiced what were called 'straights' which consisted of starting from one end of the 'drome, taking off, climbing to 20 feet then landing before we reached the other end of the 'drome. When we had mastered landings we were taken up to about 500 feet to perform figure 8's over the aerodrome. We never used much rudder on this operation being content to bank the plane a little by moving the 'joystick' to the right or the left. This action of the stick in all other planes operated the ailerons but in those old fashioned Caudrons the trailing edges of the two wings were made to warp slightly. This had the same effect i.e. it caused the plane to bank. This banking was quite enough to turn the plane gently and that was why we avoided putting any pressure on the rudder which if exaggerated could get a novice into trouble.

Eventually I was allowed to go solo on 'straights'. Afterwards I soloed on figure 8's but was allowed to do only one circuit; any more might have been dangerous.

As I was about to land from a figure 8, I realized that I would crash into a hedge as soon as I had touched down. So for the first time I gave the rudder a good kick. The result was the plane did a flat turn a few feet above the ground (most dangerous!) but I was at any rate able to land in the right direction.

I should like to explain one or two more events. Between the planes on each side we had two sets of. piano wires. The ones like these were called 'landing wires'.

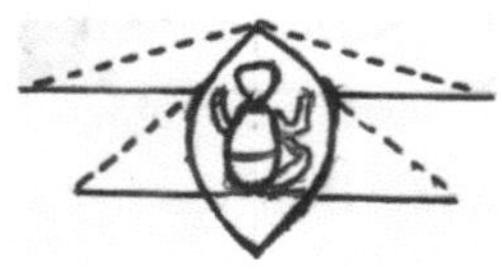

As can be seen they took the weight of the wings when on the ground. The other wires like these, were called flying wires.

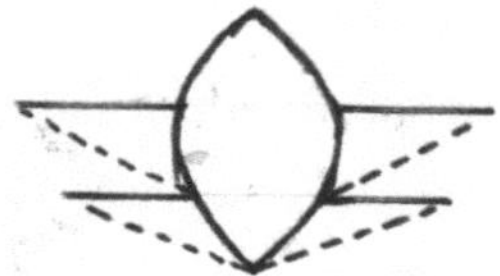

These wires took the strain when the machine was in flight.

Whenever a plane was badly landed the landing wires broke. In all other squadrons where I served the broken wires were completely replaced. But these 'froggies' took a pair of pliers from their pockets and twisted the two broken ends together again. I thought it was pretty dangerous treatment at first until I realized that the landing wires were of no importance while you were in the air. When my solo flights had been completed I applied for and was accepted as a Member of the Aero Club of the United Kingdom. I still have my membership ticket numbered 4915 of 17th June 1917. It seems a fairly low number.

We only had one accident while I was at Acton. One of the trainees was living with his wife somewhere in the town of Acton. She was generally around the aerodrome when her husband was under instruction and if he was not in sight was quite prepared to flirt with some of the officers. He was killed on a solo flight and some of us were very disgusted when a few days later, we saw her flirting again.

~

From Acton I was sent to a proper Flying Corps Training Squadron at Narborough in Norfolk. It was in a very lonely place and as a result there was nothing much to do when off duty. I remember going for a walk with some fellow officers on a very hot day. We came across an attractive pond so we all stripped and bathed in the nude. The man with whom I shared a room in a long hut could always find something to do. In private life he was on the Variety Stage and called himself a Light Comedian. He was absolutely without morals but nevertheless a very companionable fellow. He came back to camp one night very proud of the fact that he had been able to seduce a village maiden. But a few days later he discovered that he had got gonorrhoea. He was furious about this but I will not repeat what he said about the girl he had thought was a virgin. It was not his first infection because he always carried around with him some lotion which did not cure but held the disease in check. His plan was to continue using this stuff until he had qualified as a pilot and was about to be sent on active service. He would then disclose his condition to a doctor and perhaps postpone indefinitely his transfer overseas. He was quite blatant about his plans. What worried me though was that he had lost his razor and borrowed my safety razor every morning. I don't know whether there was any risk but I always soaped my razor heavily in hopes of sterilizing it before use. I was moreover very careful not to cut myself.

At Narborough there were three flights in the Squadron. In 'A' flight we learnt to fly Avros, in 'B' flight we learned on BE2c's, BE2d's and BE2e's. I don't remember now what the differences were between the three machines but you were supposed to have become more proficient when you reached BE2e's. All these types of machines had once been operational in France. In 'C' Flight we learnt to fly R.E.8's which were the machines I was to fly in France. I had three short flights as a passenger in R.E.'s before going solo. I was the first passenger my instructor had ever flown. He did not tell me that at the time but he did when I met him somewhere a year later.

I made fourteen solo flights on R.E.'s mostly for thirty or forty minutes. My total flying time on these machines before acquiring my 'wings' as a qualified pilot was eight and a half hours, during which time I passed bombing and photography tests. I also made a cross country flight in which I had to land at Kings Lynn, Sedgeford and Norwich. In one flight it is recorded that for the first time I reached 11,500 feet over the Wash. On 22nd August 1917 on my 13th Flight (as might be expected), my engine conked out when I was about 3,000 feet up and two miles or so from the aerodrome. I started to glide down and as I approached the aerodrome I decided that I could not quite make it. I decided to land in a field of mustard alongside the aerodrome which I managed to do without breaking my undercarriage. The C.O. on coming out to see if there was any damage (which there was not) said 'Pity you did not make the 'drome'. I said 'I considered I might not make it Sir and thought it better to make sure of a good landing'. All he then said was 'Probably wise'. As a matter of fact if I had had more experience I could have got the plane back without difficulty. What I had done wrong was to glide down too steeply and so approach ground level too soon.

I was under instruction at Narborough on my 21st birthday – 28th August 1917. I see that the records for that date are marked 'inclement weather', so I did not fly. About this time I was anxious to get leave since I had not been home during my six months in the Army. To my surprise I was granted what was called 3 days leave. I was to leave for home on the Saturday morning and to be back in camp on Monday evening. As it was a difficult cross-country journey to get to Warrington, with changes at four stations, most of both the Saturday and Monday would be spent in travelling. So as there was nothing for me to do on the Friday in camp I cleared off early that morning. Unfortunately I had bad luck and bumped into the C.O. while I was changing trains at Kings Lynn. The C.O. (a Major) had done at least one spell of flying in France but he was very young, inexperienced and nervous. In fact from what I saw of him I decided he left all the work to the Adjutant who was a much older and experienced man but a real martinet. It was noticeable in the Squadron Office that the C.O. sat at his desk with nothing to do while the Adjutant was overburdened with work. He must have told the Adjutant that he had seen me leaving by train because when I arrived home on Friday evening there was a telegram waiting for me saying 'Return at once'. My Mother was terribly alarmed especially when I told her that I was ordered to return because I had left a day too soon. I wanted to stay until the Monday but to pacify her I left on the Saturday morning. When I reported back to the Orderly Room I was confined to camp for a week. As there was nowhere else to go that was not much of a punishment.

Shortly after this I was granted my 'wings' and posted to Brooklands in Surrey.

Fédération Aéronautique Internationale
British Empire

We the undersigned, recognised by the F.A.I. as the sporting authority in the British Empire certify that

Nous soussignés pouvoir sportif reconnu par la F.A.I. pour l'Empire Britannique certifions que

2nd Lt Walter Crowther Balmford R.F.C.

Born at Harrington on the 28th Aug 1896.

having fulfilled all the conditions stipulated by the F.A.I. has been granted an

ayant rempli toutes les conditions imposées par la F.A.I. a été breveté

AVIATOR'S CERTIFICATE. PILOTE - AVIATEUR.

THE ROYAL AERO CLUB OF THE UNITED KINGDOM.

Chairman

Secretary

Date 17th June 1917 No 4915.

ROYAL AERO CLUB OF THE UNITED KINGDOM, CLIFFORD ST, LONDON, W.

(Signature of Holder)

Walter gets his wings, Walter's Aviator's Certificate, issued by the Royal Aero Club of the United Kingdom 17 June 1917 to Walter Balmford, 2nd Lieutenant Royal Flying Corps – 10 months before the Royal Air Force was created.

Brooklands was a motor racing track with a large flat area inside the circuit. This flat area was being used as an aerodrome. Shortly after my arrival I saw the famous aviator Hawker take a new plane up for a test flight. Apart from its use for testing purposes the place was mainly used to train pilots for spotting and reporting by wireless to the Artillery the points where shells had burst. At Brooklands of course the flashing of the guns and the bursting of the shells would be represented by artificial flashes of light. I was happily given weekend leave on arrival, so I dashed home for one night. On my return for duty on the Monday morning I was sent up to learn my way around the district before actually starting on the course. Well! I got hopelessly lost. I don't know why, because I remember seeing Staines Reservoir and I am surprised that I could not find my way from there. So I landed alongside a building site where some men were at work. I found the foreman, who was a very intelligent man, and he showed me on my map where I was. My difficulty was to know how to get off again. I could not let anybody else swing the propeller to start the engine, so I persuaded the foreman to sit in the plane with the throttle fully open and instructed him to hold the stick right back in his stomach and to pull the throttle to low as soon as the engine started. He did take his place in the pilot's seat and the workmen whom I had detailed to hold on to the plane jeered, laughed and called out good-byes. Anyway he did all that I asked when the engine started. I thanked him and his mates before I took off. I was quickly back at Brooklands and there I found a message telling me to report to the Orderly Room. Here I was told to report at the Air Board in London, the next day, with a view to proceeding to France. So I never even started my course at Brooklands. One other man received similar instructions. His name was Zinc. Once again the Army had obviously picked the first and last names from the list of new arrivals for the course. This sort of thing had happened on other occasions, sometimes with highly acceptable results but sometimes not at all satisfactory.

I remember very little of my life at Brooklands. Of course I was only there a short time. Friday night I slept in the officers' quarters, Saturday night I was at home, and then I was back again at Brooklands on the Sunday night. I have not the vaguest recollection of the mess and sleeping quarters for the trainee officers. I do remember one thing though. On the Friday, after arrival, I had gone over to (I think) either Weybridge or Surbiton to hire a bicycle. This bicycle was intended for transport between the officers' quarters and the aerodrome. As I was ordered to leave at such short notice I was unable to return the bicycle to its owner. I therefore arranged with another officer to retain the machine for the rest of the week on the understanding that he would return it to the shop from which I had hired it. After my arrival in France I wrote to the shop to enquire whether the bicycle had been returned. It had not, so I offered to compensate the owner. He was so surprised at my honesty that he let me off with £1. (It was a pretty old thing though.)

The next day I travelled to London and reported to the Air Board. I told the officer to whom I reported that I had not had a period of leave in the seven months I had been in the Army. Everybody was supposed to have what was called embarkation leave. He was somewhat sympathetic and told me to report back in two hours. When I did, he expressed his regrets and said I would have to go to France the next morning. I later learnt that casualties had been very heavy in France and that the authorities needed all the replacements they could get. I stayed this last night at the Hotel Rubens near Buckingham Palace. Next morning when I got round to Victoria Station about eight o'clock the place was packed with people returning to France. Not having been forewarned I found myself conscripted as a duty officer for the whole of the way to Boulogne. The duties were not very onerous either on the train or the boat crossing to France. In fact all I remember doing is having to ensure that people kept their lifebelts on while crossing the Straits of Dover from Folkestone.

~

On landing at Boulogne we went straight to the train drawn alongside the quay. We travelled throughout the night until we eventually reached Candas near Doullens. After sunrise I remember being struck by

(1) wagons labelled 20 hommes,
10 chevaux,

(2) long straight tree lined roads,

(3) railway stations without raised platforms and the steep climb up to the carriage doors,

(4) the dress, behaviour, gesticulations, and chatter of the locals at the stations where we stopped.

On arrival at Candas we were taken by tender to a camp of huts alongside an aerodrome to which smashed planes were returned for salvage and new ones brought from England. The repaired planes and the new ones were despatched to the various squadrons in the area.

My recollection is that about 20 officers arrived together to find about 30 others already there. It was called a 'Pilots' Pool' and although on looking back it seems as though it ought to have been a demoralizing experience there, I don't think we were at all concerned at the time. It was a very idle life. To keep us occupied we were supposed to salvage parts from the damaged planes that had been brought in but there was no drive to do any work and no supervision. I don't think any of us did very much work. Another feature that might have been depressing had we not been immune was that every day one or two officers would be taken away to various squadrons which were in need of new pilots. We knew very well that they were replacements of casualties. I remember feeling a little concerned when eight of us were all taken off together to the same squadron, No.6, on the Ypres front. We knew Ypres was a hot spot but eight in one day!

Except for one thing, I remember very little of the life we led in the Pilots' Pool where we were stuck for about a week. The thing I remember is the little French boys who, every afternoon at about 4 o'clock came round the camp selling the Continental Edition of the *Daily Mail* which was printed in Paris. They went to the entrance of each hut calling out 'Daily Mail. Dirtee Book'.

The eight of us posted to No.6 Squadron left after dinner in the mess and were taken with our baggage by tender on a sixty-mile journey to a place called Abele just over the border in Belgium. We did not arrive there until about midnight. I still recall vividly that weird drive on a very black night. The sky was continually lit by flashes of gun fire ahead. I suppose our starting point was about 70 miles from the front line. I remember we stopped at some place, probably Hazebrouck, for something to eat. The Town Mayor was having a meal in the cafe. He was a chatty fellow but he made himself look ridiculous to us by telling us that we should thank him for suggesting to some aircraft manufacturer that planes should be fitted with a clutch. He could hardly believe us when we assured him that no plane was, nor ever had been, fitted with a clutch.

There were three flights in No.6 Squadron. I was allotted to 'B' Flight. The C.O. of the Squadron was Major Archibald James who had been educated at Eton and Cambridge. He had joined the Flying Corps in France in 1915 and had been awarded the Military Cross for bringing a damaged plane back to base. It may have been an unusual feat in the early days of the War but it wasn't in my time. I don't wish to belittle his effort in the slightest but people no longer got the Military Cross for such adventures. In fact after an encounter, which I describe later, in which my plane was badly mauled, my Flight Commander pressed the C.O. to recommend me for the M.C. because I had safely brought a severely damaged plane to the ground and saved the life of my badly wounded observer. But the C.O. maintained that I was only doing my job – which was correct.

Major James regarded himself as an aristocrat. He did not mix with us very much and always went off to his hut after his dinner in 'B' Flight mess. But he was keen, fair and thorough in his job. He never showed his real feelings about us middle class blokes. I did, however, have three brushes with him.

~

The first brush was while we were at Abele. One night the Germans made a very heavy raid on our aerodrome in the course of which a bomb fell between two large huts in each of which about twenty men were sleeping. There were horrible shambles. But what upset me was that after some dead bodies had been pulled out the C.O. ordered them to be thrown into a hastily-dug common grave. I expressed my disgust because, as I said, men killed in the front line were, if possible, given a proper individual burial by a chaplain. The C.O. probably decided to take this action to save the morale of the others. I believe now he may have been right.

The next brush with the C.O. occurred when the Squadron was at Bertangles where we were stationed after leaving Abele. On several occasions men reported having seen a wild boar run across a corner of the aerodrome. There were some doubts about the reliability of these stories until a sentry, on night duty, on the aerodrome, was definitely knocked down by a wild boar. As a result the C.O. ordered a boar hunt. He invited the General who was in charge of our area (I don't remember what his command was called) and two of our officers to participate in the hunt. The C.O. of course was to be with the guns. The rest of the officers in the Squadron were detailed to act as beaters. None of us was very keen on this because we thought it likely we would miss the fun. I tried to solve this problem by going to the armoury and getting a revolver which I thought might be useful if I encountered the boar. We were entitled to take the revolvers and use them on the target range. If the corporal in the gun room suspected why I wanted the revolver, he could not refuse to let me have it. He did however report the matter to the C.O. who immediately sent for me. I agreed when he asked me if I proposed to take the revolver on the beat. He said it was a most dangerous procedure for a beater to be armed and ordered me to return the revolver to the gun room which I did. I again have to admit that he was right in taking the action he did.

As I have started this story I might as well finish it here instead of later on where it belongs.

The next day we beaters set out and tramped for miles along organized routes – but saw nothing. This should have been the end of the story but it had an extraordinary sequel. One of the officers in my Flight borrowed my plane to do a job because his was out of action. When he returned he reported to my mechanic that a strut between the upper and lower planes was cracked and that he had seen the crack open a little when doing a turn. My rigger and I made a very careful check of the strut but decided there was nothing wrong. I then decided to take the plane up myself to see if I could detect a fault. After manoeuvring around a bit I decided that it was the sun's rays shining on the strut which created an illusion. I was, at the time, over the aerodrome and on looking down I saw a lot of people running across a nearby field. I had no idea why they should be doing this, but on landing I was told the boar had just run across the aerodrome and that the C.O. was after it with a gun. As a matter of fact he shot it. It looked a magnificent specimen when I saw it being carried towards the cook house. It seemed extraordinary that the killing should have occurred on the very next day after an organized hunt had failed to find it. Anyway a few days later we had a glorious feast of roast boar.

Before it was cooked however, the local Lord of the Manor (Le Châtelain, I suppose) turned up. I had never seen him before but I knew of his existence because I had explored his estate and ventured up to the large rather dilapidated château where he lived. I suppose an ancestor of his had been banished there whenever Louis XIV had got fed up with him at Court. It appeared that he had certain rights over boars in his demesne and had come to protest about the shooting. The C.O. turned on all his charms, invited him to come into the mess for lunch, and was forgiven for his misdemeanour. But we did not give him any boar to eat.

The last story has been rather long. I have still to recount the details of my third brush with the C.O. It occurred when we were at Le Crotoy at the mouth of the Somme. The C.O. had been promoted to Wing Commander and the day before leaving the Squadron he threw a dinner at the local hotel for the officers. He invited everyone individually except me and one of the observers Lt. Clark. We both took offence at this, even though he did ask someone to tell me that I was invited.

Neither Clark nor I attended the dinner and the next day the C.O. asked me why I did not turn up. I gave my reason, to which he replied that he had asked so and so to tell me. Once again he may have been in the right. I must have been a troublesome person in those days (perhaps I still am) because I have had to admit that in each of three brushes with the C.O. he had some right on his side.

I have, after a long diversion, to return to the time of my arrival at No.6 Squadron at Abele. On each of the first two days there I flew for forty minutes around the 'drome. It was necessary for me to familiarize myself with the countryside so that I could quickly find my way back to base. It was also desirable that I should get to know the idiosyncrasies (if any) of the machine I had been allotted. It was an R.E.8, a type which I had learnt to fly in England. All the machines in the Squadron had a large letter painted on both sides of the fuselage so that we could identify one another in the air. Mine had 'V' (called Vic) which I now regard as being the forerunner of 'V' for Victory. The 'R.E.' in the name of the type of plane stood for 'Reconnaissance Experimental'. This type of machine, a two-seater had been designed in the Royal Aircraft Factory. It was generally regarded by most of the Flying Corps as a dangerous machine to fly and too slow for its job. But I would never listen to any criticism of R.E.8's because 'Vic' behaved itself very well for me.

The work of the Squadron was mainly:

(1) what we called 'a shoot' (i.e. reporting by wireless to the artillery where a shell had fallen),

(2) photography behind the enemy lines,

(3) 'spark control' (i.e. observing the position of enemy guns from the flashes when they fired),

(4) short distance bombing,

(5) contact patrol (i.e. flying close to the ground and noting during an attack the position of the infantry, both ours and the Germans, and receiving messages from below by signal lamps or sending them by dropping bags).

As I said earlier, there were three flights in the Squadron and I was in 'B' Flight. We were concerned with all the above activities, except No.5, which was the most hazardous of the lot. Contact Patrol was usually assigned to 'C' Flight. During an attack by our infantry the artillery on both sides put up a barrage behind their opponent's trenches.

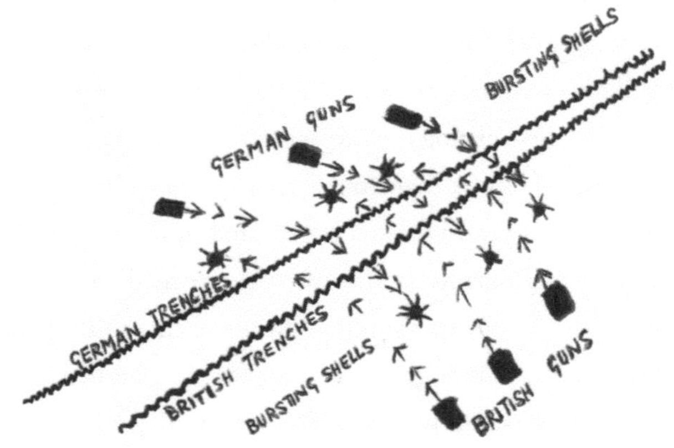

As can be seen from the rather crude sketch the two barrages created a corridor around the trenches which was free of bursting shells. The unfortunate members of 'C' Flight had to enter the corridor at one end and fly low (100 to 300 feet) to do their job. Their only consolation was that, if there were any Huns in the corridor, each side was too busy to attack the other. During such an attack as this we others would be doing our stuff higher up where the Hun scouts would be out in force waiting to pounce on us.

On looking through my Pilot's Log Book it is surprising to see how often at this time we ran into bad weather or struck engine trouble. Either event caused us to endeavour to hurry back to base if we thought we could make it. But torrential rain or a spluttering engine forced us to land in the safest place we could find. This would often be on another squadron's aerodrome but sometimes in a field.

Around this time too, our aerodrome was frequently subject to heavy bombing, usually at night when we were in bed. In the first few attacks I was inclined to get up and watch the progress of the raid. But I remember one night, when I was caught unawares, I woke up to hear a bomb explosion followed by another one a little nearer to me. There were five bombs in succession each one sounding nearer and the last one perilously close. The blast of the fifth bomb was followed by the whine of another descending bomb. 'This is it' I thought and I automatically pulled the blankets over my head for protection. The blankets would not have done much good but fortunately the next sound I heard was the squelch of a dud bomb dropping in a farmyard pond about 30 yards from my hut.

I would like to tell about one veteran in our Squadron whose name I have forgotten. His first exploit was to serve from the landing in Gallipoli until the evacuation. He was then transferred to France where he served in the infantry for about a year. He then transferred to the Royal Flying Corps and, after training in England as an observer, returned to active service in France for, I suppose, about six months. On his return to England he did a pilot's course in flying and then joined our squadron in France. Altogether he had been at the thick of things practically continuously from early 1915 to the end of 1917. I learnt his history shortly after my arrival in No.6 Squadron. But what amazed me was that he was the first man to get out of bed and away as soon as he realized that the Germans were circulating round our aerodrome in readiness for an attack. He did not move just outside our huts but got three hundred yards or more away. I know how far he went because when I had, like him, learnt a little sense from experience, I used to go with him.

~

It is unfortunate that, although we were certainly not taught any aerial strategy, we were given little guidance in tactics in aerial combat. A few brilliant officers who had survived several combats worked out very successfully their own tactics. But ours was not a fighter squadron and we pilots needed more instruction on how to defend ourselves. So far as I can recall we were only taught a few things

(1) Never to fly straight when attacked because you became a sitting target for the enemy. My first encounter occurred when I was returning from a 'shoot' in the dusk – a most dangerous time especially with the wind, as it usually was when flying west against you. As the Germans dived on my rear I tossed my plane from side to side fairly rapidly. But when we got down (my first night landing in the dark without, of course, any landing lights) my observer complained that as a result of my frequent swerving he could not keep his guns in line with the attacking aircraft (four albatross scouts according to my log book). However I had been rightly more concerned to keep out of their sights than to help my observer to get his sights in line.

(2) Never to dive in order to escape from an enemy scout (nowadays called a fighter) because the excess of his speed over that of an R.E.8 was much greater in a dive than when flying level.

(3) If 3 planes were flying in formation like this

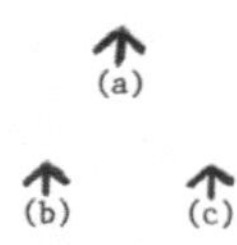

and leader (a) turned to the right quickly, (b), having to travel in a much larger circle, would be left a long way behind and well out on the left. The proper tactic was for (a) to turn slowly and thus enable both (b) and (c) to maintain their positions relative to (a). I describe later how I was the one, in a desperate situation, to be left out on a limb with dire consequences.

As a matter of fact I was always much happier as the leader in position (a) during a bombing or photographic raid. When I was behind the leader I was always wondering whether he had noticed the enemy planes several miles away and what he was going to do, either go on or turn back and if the latter would he turn to the left or the right. As a leader my mind was fully occupied with these and other matters so I was not worried at all.

I remember on one occasion when I was leading a bombing raid our target was a wood about 15 miles beyond the lines (i.e. trenches). The wood was supposed to be occupied by horse lines. The whole of my attention was directed to the various problems and when I looked down I suddenly thought I saw the wood almost below. We carried 6 bombs under the fuselage. Three bombs were released together by pulling a lever. Each of the other bombs was released singly by pulling another lever three times. I let all 3 bombs go and to my horror saw that I was aiming at the wrong wood. So I signalled to my companions not to drop their bombs. Then I thought I might as well watch the descent of my bombs. You could follow them all the way to the ground because their forward speed was the same as that of the plane.

It was quite a fascinating sight to watch them twisting and turning on the way down. I realized that they were going to hit the wood I had seen but, believe it or not, they were heading for a German balloon parked in the middle of the wood. They arrived pretty close to the balloon and it burst into flames. I reported this when I got back to base and honestly reported that the destruction was a complete fluke. The next day, in what we called 'Comic Cuts', which used to give daily details of what the various squadrons had done, there was a paragraph which read 'Lt Balmford, while leading a flight over enemy lines, observed a German balloon on the ground, bombed it and destroyed it'. I suppose the writer thought that his version would give a greater boost to morale.

Now for my story of the raid in which, from my point of view, the leader turned the wrong way too quickly. I have always imagined that it took place on 11 November 1917 (a year before the Armistice) but I see from my log book that it was the 12th. Three of us had been over in the morning taking photos of the ground behind the enemy lines. We were attacked by 9 Albatross Scouts of which my gunner, Corporal Elliott, shot one down. The result of that interruption was that our mission was incomplete and we had to return in the afternoon to take the area which had not been photographed. My log book records that on this occasion we were twice attacked by '6 Huns' without saying what sort. I don't remember what happened in the first attack but we must have shaken them off by some means because we again headed east to complete our photography. They came at us from the front, fast and furious this time. I was behind the leader on his left and when he made a sharp turn to the right in order to return to our side of the lines, I was left hopelessly behind. The result was the Huns concentrated on me while I was without fire support from the other two planes. Immediately my landing wires were shot away though fortunately my flying wires remained intact. (I have explained what these wires were in the section dealing with my first flights in a Caudron.) The next to go were the wires connected to the ailerons and the elevator. The result was the joy stick which operated these controls was slack and floppy. I could not bank to the left or the right nor force the plane to go up or down. Fortunately my rudder controls remained intact. If these had gone I would not have been able to steer the plane and, as it had a natural tendency to swing to the right, it would have quickly got into a spin and crashed. Two other things happened. I suddenly saw a small round bullet hole appear in the mica windscreen about a foot from my nose – most alarming I can tell you. The other thing was that when Corporal Elliott who was behind me tapped me on the shoulder I looked around and saw his face covered in blood. He pointed to his machine gun which had been smashed by bullets in several places and said 'I think I downed another'. The plain fact was that my life had been saved because Elliott was between me and the German guns.

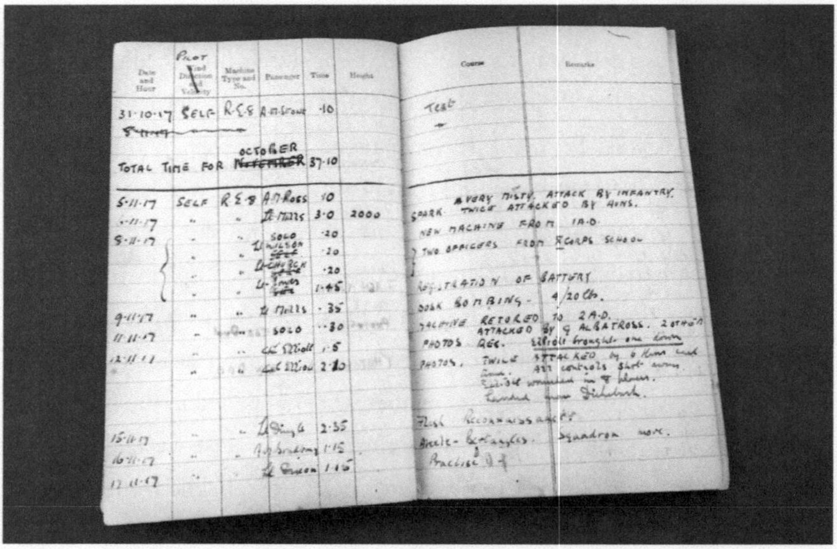

A page from Walter's log book – including the day he was shot down, his gunner Corporal Elliott was injured, and Walter landed the plane safely.

My problem was how to get the plane down in such a disabled condition. The plane had started to enter a spinning dive but fortunately I was able to correct that with my rudder. It was during this spinning dive that I realized how true it was that in moments of extreme tension and peril one has vivid visions of one's past life and loses control of one's bodily functions. I then entered into a fairly steep dive to our lines and when about 200 feet above the ground I levelled off the plane. Without an elevator I was able to do this with a device which was used when landing to help to get the rear of the plane down and the nose up. I had in fact got some sort of elevator control. Having got the plane into horizontal flight at about two hundred feet I continued until I had crossed the trenches and the area full of shell holes where no plane could land. I very soon saw a decent patch of flat land ahead where I thought with Elliott badly wounded, it would be better to land rather than to struggle back to the aerodrome about 15 miles away. I didn't go into any details about the device I referred to earlier but I must explain the next trick which I had up my sleeve and decided to use. In the following diagram BA represents the line of a plane gliding downwards. AC represents the line of pull of the engine if switched on. The secret of landing is that when gliding down near to the earth you keep operating the elevator so as to pull the nose up. In other words you try not to land and, at the same time, to lose flying speed. If this is done properly the plane gradually sinks on to the ground instead of into it.

Well as I came into land with my engine just ticking over but no elevator control, I waited until almost the last moment and then gave the engine a sudden short burst of power which switched the angle of diving to

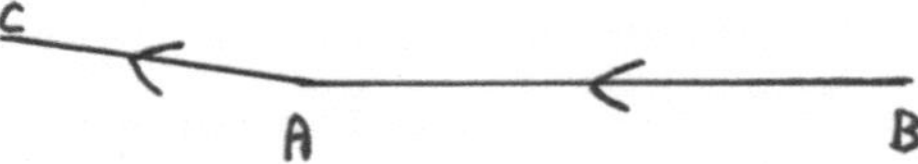

and I could thus slowly settle on to the ground. Some people might think it showed great skill but I had never tried to do it before. There was more good luck about it than anything else because I did settle on to the ground and did not even smash my undercarriage which was the usual result of a bad landing.

I had landed beside an Australian battery of field guns. A stretcher and ambulance were quickly obtained and Elliott was carried off to hospital. I wrote to him shortly afterwards and in his reply he told me that although the head injury from which the blood was flowing was not at all serious he had eight bullet wounds in his body and had lost his leg.

My next job was to phone the Squadron to tell them that I was safe and that the plane was badly damaged. They were very relieved because my comrades had given me up for lost. They promised to send a truck round the next day with a party of men to get the plane away. I was able to give them the exact pinpoint on the map where they would find me.

I was then taken round to the officers' mess, given a whisky and examined by their doctor. I had dinner in the mess and spent the night on a bed in a dug-out. I noticed that the doctor was watching me very closely all the evening. Later he told me I ought not to fly again without a medical examination. He gave me a letter to that effect. I never handed the letter in and kept it for many years. I can't make out where it is now.

The truck arrived early the next morning. The sergeant in charge did not know how I had managed to make a safe landing in such a damaged plane. I rode back to our aerodrome in the front of the truck. After reporting to the Squadron office I did what was considered the best thing for anyone who might be suffering from shock. I got hold of another plane and had a short flip around.

I have always said that it was the German Ace Richthofen who shot me down on this occasion. But I have no evidence to prove this. We knew that his squadron was operating on the same front as we were and that its planes were all painted in bright colours – like Paris hat boxes we said. And it was certainly some of those hat boxes that attacked me. Richthofen was shot down at a spot quite close to Bertangles where we were later stationed. I walked over there and saw the remains of his crashed plane.

Ever since then there have been disputes as to whether he was shot down by the Canadian airman who was chasing him or by an Australian gunner on the ground firing a machine gun. We in the Air Force firmly believed that he was shot down by the Canadian. Years later, in Australia, I became very friendly with Major General Beavis who was the major in charge of the battery alongside which Richthofen fell. Beavis was convinced that his man had brought the airman down and we had many arguments about it because it is extremely difficult to hit a plane from the ground. My own theory is that the German had been badly injured during combat with the Canadian. Why else would he have been so close to the ground? At the time he appeared over the battery he was desperately trying to find somewhere to land. At the crucial moment he fainted from his wounds and the plane crashed into the ground.

I remember one night about this time returning to our aerodrome at Abele in a French Army car with a French driver. I have tried hard to recall where I had been and how I came to be with a Frenchman, but I cannot. Nor have I any idea what the object of my mission had been. The only inference I can make is that I had been to some conference. What I am about to relate is a quite insignificant incident but the concluding part is so vivid in my mind that I am intrigued to know why I cannot remember the preliminary details. One other such detail in my mind's eye seems wrong because I see the driver sitting on the right hand side of the front seat and me on his left. This would not be so if the car had been of French make. The only explanation can be that the French had been supplied with some English cars.

I have said enough to suggest to a reader that if I give any further details they must be figments of my imagination. But from now on all the details have been retained vividly in my mind and I assert that they are absolutely true.

As I said we were returning to Abele (in Belgium). We had come from the direction of Hazebrouek (in France). When we reached the border between the two countries the car was stopped by a British military policeman, for inspection. He did not waste any time and quickly told us to drive on. The French driver turned to me and said (I think, if my French is correct) *Qu'est ce qu'il a dit.* Now the only point to this story is my reply which I gave instantly and without any thought. I said *en avant* and the driver went forward. The thing that intrigued me as soon as I had said it was where the expression had come from. I could not recall learning in my schooldays that *en avant!* meant 'forward!' but it quite suddenly came to me that in Dumas' book (which I had read before I was ten but not since) *The Three Musketeers* after every scrap dashed off on their horses, waving their swords and shouting *en avant.*

I admit it's not much of a story but it has always intrigued me especially as it is in line with other occasions when suddenly called upon to produce a French word I have done so at once from the unexplored recesses of my mind. If I had sat down to really think what the word was I would have been unable to do so.

Shortly after this episode the squadron left Abele and moved to Bertangles, a few miles north of Amiens. The procedure was to take all the mechanics we could with us in the planes so that they could get on with their jobs immediately upon arrival. The observers and other members of the squadron travelled in the transport trucks.

It was in the middle of November 1917 that we moved to Bertangles. We had a good life there for four months – free from the War and with many enjoyable outings in Amiens. We were to conduct a course of instruction for Infantry and Artillery officers to show them what the Flying Corps could and could not do. There had been frequent complaints by the infantry that we often failed in our job to look after their interests. The high-ups in the Flying Corps concluded that this misunderstanding was due to general ignorance about the capabilities of the Corps – hence the course of instruction. (It should be remembered that we were still part of the Army and that the criticisms were not a dispute between the Army and the Air Force.) The course was organized as follows – every week a batch of thirty or so officers arrived and were divided between the three flights. They were housed and messed in some hutments alongside our aerodrome which the squadron had not previously used.

I find from my Pilot's Log Book that during the 2½ months the course lasted I made 69 flights and carried 32 different officers made up as follows:

Brigadier Generals	4
Lt. Colonels	14
Majors	10
Captains	1
Lieutenants	3
	32

The course consisted of lectures on the first day by the C.O. our Intelligence Officer and our Gunnery Officer. Afterwards we took the visitors up on specific jobs. The first was to get them acclimatised to flying. After flying for about an hour I would hand my passenger a map, point out our present position and that of the aerodrome and ask him to guide me back. They were pretty good at that job – as might be expected. They had received instructions on how to aim a machine gun in aerial combat making due allowance for the speed and direction of both planes. Two planes would then be fitted up with camera guns. These were built something like a machine gun except that when the trigger was pressed the gun took a series of photos. The sights, with which they were aimed, were marked by a large cross and a similar mark appeared in the centre of each photo. The two planes would then engage in mock combat. If the photo showed a plane in the following position the shot would not have hit the target because the plane was flying away from the centre of the cross.

But a photo like the following indicated that the shot would probably have hit the target.

Our passengers were hopeless at this test. They usually failed to get the opposing aircraft in the picture.

Another exercise was to divide the Squadron into two opposing groups. The planes in one group carried streamers to distinguish them from their rivals.

A line between Amiens and a place about 15 miles away was supposed to represent the line dividing two opposing forces of infantry. The planes with the banners were supposed to be patrolling this line to prevent those without banners, who were about 10 miles on the other side of the line, from crossing it. This operation was one of the main objectives of the course because the infantry claimed that we were never around when the Germans crossed the lines. Well! it was just a farce. The attackers had only to hang around on their side until they could see a wide gap between two of the defending planes, and then cross over at a height well above or well below the defenders. It was of course impossible to stop the enemy getting through as was proved again in the second war before Radar came into its own.

It was during one of these episodes of 'Crossing the Line' as we called it, that a fog descended without warning over the whole area. The entire squadron was out on the operation and had to get down at once. A few lucky ones were handy to the 'drome and got home without trouble. Seven out of probably eighteen planes made forced landings in fields. Some of the occupants were injured slightly but fortunately none seriously. I was probably about 5 miles from the 'drome when the fog came down. I descended to about 100 feet above the ground and proceeded in the direction to take me back to the 'drome. I handed my map to my passenger, showed him our approximate whereabouts and told him to guide me home. Flying at such a low height in fog I needed to give my whole attention to the job. Anyway after a few minutes my passenger (Major Wilson was his name, bless him!), tapped me on the shoulder and pointed to a railway line below. We both knew that the railway ran alongside the aerodrome and that we were flying in the right direction and so we got home to glory.

When the course of instruction was over we collected a batch of newly qualified observers from England and trained them in readiness for going 'into battle' again.

A few other events at Bertangles may be of interest. I have already told about the boar hunt. Towards the end of our stay there the officers were instructed to go out and dig for victory (but I think it was called that in the second war). Food at this time (March 1918) was getting very short. The idea was that we should dig an area of ground in which vegetables could be grown. We went at it with vigour and I don't remember any complaints. But the seeds were never sown because we were forced to leave the area shortly afterwards. Anyway before our departure the President of the Mess Committee (P.M.C.) had a bright idea. He bought about a dozen baby pigs which it was proposed we should fatten up and eat. He also sent to Amiens for a veterinarian to come and castrate the pigs. The P.M.C. and I held the pigs by their hind legs for the vet. to perform his operations. The animals screamed like blazes during the operation but ran about, when released, apparently none the worse for the adventure. To complete the record though I have to relate the curious fact that both the P.M.C. and I admitted to one another afterwards that we were both suffering a sympathetic discomfort in our parts which corresponded with those that the poor pigs had lost.

It was while we were at Bertangles that the announcement was made that the Royal Flying Corps and the Royal Naval Air Service were to be combined on 1 April 1918 to form the Royal Air Force.

Our aerodrome at Bertangles was only a few miles from Amiens and we took full advantage of that. Every afternoon a tender was provided to take officers into Amiens and to bring them back some time before (I think) 11 o'clock. The men were also provided with tenders but as there were more of them they were not able to go as often as we did.

I have made notes of a number of incidents which occurred in Amiens.

On one occasion on arriving at the Station Square to meet the returning tender I found an English soldier supporting a friend who was obviously unconscious. I asked what was wrong. The man said they had been drinking wine in a French cafe and that his friend's wine had been drugged in order to rob him. He said they had got his money. The man was very concerned about his friend and particularly that he might be caught by the military police. He expected no sympathy from that quarter. I offered to take them both in my tender to a military hospital and he agreed to go. When we got there the sick man was carried and put on a bench that looked like an operating table. A doctor came straight away and after I had told him what the trouble was he pressed the man's eyelids up and said, 'Yes, he's been drugged all right'. He sent for a stomach pump and I watched this operation for a while.

In Amiens our favourite haunt for dinner was Josephines. You entered through the kitchen and walked upstairs to the dining room. Josephine knew us very well and when we arrived she would show us to her private dining room cum bed-room. I remember that the article under the bed which we used, to avoid going out in the cold, contained in the centre a realistically painted bullseye. It was a nicely furnished room and we had some wonderful meals there. It was the only French restaurant I ever visited in those days in which the plates were always hot. Before anything was served by the waitresses – no waiters of course in wartime – Josephine felt each plate to check whether it complied with her standards. If it did not she made a waitress bring some hotter ones.

I visited this restaurant again in 1921 when I was on holiday in France with Harold Emmerson. It was still there and when I entered the kitchen the fat old cook in charge cried out 'Ah – Monsieur l'officier anglais, qui m'a donné beaucoup de cigarettes pour les blessés'. It was nice to be welcomed like that and what she said was true. On leaving the restaurant we always gave her some cigarettes to pass on to wounded soldiers. But I wondered whether she said the same thing to every obvious Englishman who visited the restaurant in 1921.

I have to mention, without any shame, because I regarded it as part of my education, that we visited other places in Amiens – French brothels. It was impossible to get liquor in the recognised quarters after 9.30 p.m. in Amiens but we led a gay carefree dangerous life which made us permanently thirsty. The only places we knew where drinks could be bought (at a terrific price) were brothels. So we used to go to the brothels for an hour or so after the restaurants had closed. Let me say at once, with absolute truth and before anyone gets alarmed, that on only one occasion did one of our party, go upstairs with one of the girls – and it was not I. The usual procedure, when we arrived at the house of ill-fame, was for a slot in the front door to be opened after we had knocked. Someone looked through the gap and after deciding that we were all right, let us in. We were greeted by 'Madame' who showed us to a large room with chairs along the sides of the walls. She then took our order which of necessity was always champagne because it was all she served. By the way, the champagne was always Heidseik 1906. After the champagne had been produced the girls arrived and expected much to our annoyance to join in the champagne. I suppose they got some. They were all dressed in short slips with bare bosoms, but they did not stay in the room for long after realizing that no-one was going to succumb to their charms.

Perhaps it could be said that to make amends for this misbehaviour, two other officers and I regularly went to the opera which was produced every Sunday afternoon, at a theatre in Amiens. The music and singing were good but from the box we always occupied we got rather too close a view of the singers who, largely due to the War, were much too old for the parts they played.

~

Before I pass on from those happy days in Amiens there is one more experience I should describe. One of the most popular officers in the Squadron was a man named Longbottom (of course we always called him Shortarse). I should think I attended more dinners with him in Amiens, than anybody else. He came from Leeds and spoke very slowly with a strong Yorkshire accent. He was a lovable man. But the odd thing about him was that, although he had a very bad stammer, he had been taught how to control it. Generally when talking he seemed to know when he was approaching a difficult passage and he used to pause and wait until he knew he could master it. These pauses were most intriguing and in his way he used them for dramatic effect. Another feature was that unlike many people who become noisy and excited after they have had a few drinks, Longbottom told his stories in a low lugubrious voice. Well! at the conclusion of a meal in Amiens or in the tender on the way back to camp we nearly always called on Longbottom to tell us a story. He always told the same story in his own inimitable style and we all always enjoyed it.

The story was about a bird which he called a sparrow but which really should, for the point of the story, have been a singing bird. Anyway I will call it a sparrow. It was a cold winter's day and the snow on the ground was very thick. As a result the sparrow was very cold and miserable and had had nothing to eat for several days. It was in fact on the verge of death. And then along came a horse and cart which paused for a while beneath the branch of the tree on which the sparrow was sitting. When the horse and cart had moved on the sparrow was delighted to see that a beautiful heap of steaming hot manure had been left behind. The sparrow immediately swooped down and enjoyed to the full this beautiful gift from heaven. When it could eat no more it flew back on to its branch and started to sing and chirp to its heart's content in order to display its thanks to God for his mercy. At this moment along came a man with a gun who also was feeling very cold and miserable just like the sparrow had been. Suddenly he heard the sparrow's song and, on looking up, shot the poor sparrow dead.

I heard that story so many times that I believe I have told it more or less in Longbottom's own words. It was at this point too, that anybody else who had not heard the story before, was wondering what the point of the story was. After quite a long pause Longbottom would say

'Well! you see, there is a moral to that story' (another pause) 'If you do have to eat shit' (another very long pause and then a controlled rush of words) 'Don't make a song about it'.

If any reader thinks that story is not funny, or too vulgar, he has not appreciated the circumstances and manner in which it was told.

The last time I saw Longbottom was in a military hospital at Hampstead (London). He had been wounded in his buttock (much to his disgust) and invalided home. But he was still chirpy. I wonder if he ever tells his famous story now. If he doesn't I'll bet he has got another almost as good.

~

Well! of course all good times come to an end, and the bad times return. What had happened was that the Germans had started a massive attack on 21st March 1918 and had very quickly driven the British forces back on the Somme front almost to Amiens. (I know that most of Amiens was evacuated because I went there one day during the crisis to collect a tunic I had left to be repaired. The shop where I had left it was boarded up and there was no-one inside. So I never saw my tunic again.) This retreat was on our doorstep. Several of us in the Squadron were given tenders and told to go and find suitable landing grounds in readiness for a movement to the rear by the Flying Corps (why something like this had not been done before I do not know). On my return I was sent to Air Force Headquarters to report to General Brooke-Popham. (He became well known as the Air Force Commander in Singapore before it fell in February 1942.) Popham gave me a stack of red flags and the pinpoints of the places to which various Squadrons were to retire. My instructions were to place these flags at any awkward spots on the proposed sites for the benefit of aircraft landing there.

These were exciting times. We suddenly got orders to clear out of Bertangles because, as our squadron had not yet been brought back to fighting strength our aerodrome was needed for other operational squadrons. In fact three squadrons arrived immediately after we left. I never heard whether they enjoyed the pigs we had castrated.

Our instructions were to proceed to Le Crotoy at the mouth of the Somme. The landing place was the sandy shore of the estuary if the tide was not too high. Fortunately there was a small aerodrome inland which we could use if we were caught by a high tide, but it was none too big. We did have to use it occasionally. There was also a French Training Squadron at Le Crotoy but I don't remember that we ever fraternised with the people there except for an officer called 'Un Aspirant'. In the British Navy he would have been called a midshipman but he was not a boy. He spoke quite good English and was the liaison officer between us and the French Squadron.

At this time I was Acting but unpaid Flight Commander because the Captain was on leave in England. It was thus my job to organize the move of 'B' Flight. Fortunately I had had the experience of the move from Abele to Bertangles so I had a pretty good idea as to what had to be done.

We all arrived safely at Le Crotoy on 26 March 1918 and experienced our first landing on a sandy shore. It had been decided that as there were no available huts, we should be billetted in the town. According to my ticket I was to go to M. Le Curé. My observer Lt. Gerry Barre had been given a ticket to go to Mlle Marguerite. His billet sounded more attractive to me and my billet appealed more to him because he was a Catholic from a place about 40 miles south of Belfast, where 'The Mountains of Mourne roll down to the sea'. He loved those mountains and having a good tenor voice would gladly sing the song about them when he had had a few drinks. He and I operated together for just over two months until I was invalided home. It was a sad day when I read in *The Times* that he had been killed in an attack by the British forces on 10 August 1918 along with several other members of my old No.6. Squadron. I even felt that if I had stayed in the Squadron I could have kept him out of trouble. Well, as we both coveted the other's billetting ticket, we did a swop. Barre was happy with the Parish priest and each evening on returning, helped Le Curé to dispose of his cognac. From my point of view it was also a fortunate exchange. Mlle Marguerite turned out to be Madame Marguerite. She lived in a house attached to a wine shop in the main street of the town. The business was being managed by her husband on behalf of her son-in-law who was away at the War. Living in the house were Jeanne Lejeune, their elder married daughter and her son Georges aged four. Another daughter Alice was there, who, if things had been normal, would have been living in Boulogne with her parents the Marguerites. During the period I was living with these people, I got to know them very well. After the War in 1921, I returned to Le Crotoy and stayed with Mme Lejeune and her husband. Harold Emmerson was with me. He and I stayed for two nights and then moved on to Amiens which we explored and thence on to Paris.

The two girls had finished their education at a school in Brighton and so could speak English fairly well. When I returned to my billet, I also was regaled with café cognac with the whole family. After the father went to bed the mother would not leave me alone with her two daughters – not that I was waiting for her to do so. But for the most part it must have been a dreary evening for her because she was very deaf and did not understand a word of English. The girls were glad to practise their English on me and I certainly improved my knowledge of colloquial French. They laughed uproariously at my pronunciation of 'grenouille' (frog) but I retaliated by asking them to repeat 'Mrs Thistlewaite of Oswaldtwisle.' I don't know why but on one occasion I wanted to refer to a 'slim waist', but I could not think of the word for 'slim'. So I switched to a 'tightly laced waist' which I translated as 'une taille beaucoup pressé'. When I said this both girls went into fits of laughter and I realized that to them it must have meant 'a waist much squeezed or cuddled'. When the laughter subsided they explained that I should have said 'une taille d'une abeille' (a bee's waist). But it was beyond Mme Marguerite's ability to pronounce even 'hot'. She sat up straight, took a deep breath, paused and then said 'ot'. One night after I had been there for some time, the Germans raided the town and our landing place on the shore. I got up, called the family and, carrying the infant, led the way down to the extensive wine cellars under the house and shop. We must have stayed there in our night attire for nearly two hours until the firing of the anti-aircraft guns ceased. It was after that evening, when the mother firmly believed that I had saved the whole family by getting them into a safe place, that she relaxed her vigil over the two girls and left them to my tender mercies until long after she had gone to bed. The old lady showed that she trusted me and I have appreciated her gesture ever since.

We spent almost a month doing practical operations with our new observers and getting to know them. It was during this period that Barre and I became close friends and developed complete confidence in one another's ability. When not on duty we went for long walks together around the countryside. After a while two flights (of which my 'B' flight was one) were moved to Auxi-le-Château to engage in short distance bombing. The Flight that remained at Le Crotoy replaced one of the others a little later and so on every week. There seemed to be very few enemy aircraft about at Auxi-le-Château as compared with what we had had to put up with when operating from Abele. In fact there is only one incident recorded in my Pilot's Log Book. It says I led a formation which 'attacked 8 enemy aircraft'. I can't believe it. It must be a mistake for 'attacked by 8 enemy aircraft'. I have no recollection of ever attacking any German aircraft. We could not afford to do so because they were much faster and could manoeuvre much better than we could. I do remember that on a similar mission of which I was not a member, our chaps, on emerging from a cloud, came upon a bunch of German planes. The Germans must have been trainees on a practice flight because our leader shot two planes down with his front gun and his observer downed 3 more. There was great excitement in the Squadron when they returned. Both the pilot and the observer were awarded the M.C. In fact the observer became a flight commander which as far as I know had never happened before.

By this time the main German attack on the Somme had ended, but I well remember our C.O. reading to us a message to the troops from Sir Douglas Haig (the General Officer commanding the British) exhorting us to fight with our backs to the wall. But plans were being made for an attack against the Germans on a wide front. I knew this because the Squadron was directed to prepare for carrying out 'contact patrol' operations with the cavalry. In order that we should get to know one another, some officers were sent to live with cavalry regiments for a week. (Barre went to one but was not happy because they were such a snobbish lot and regarded themselves as the élite.) Cavalry officers visited our mess and each evening they sent along horses for us to ride around on. We took these officers up above for trips. All these arrangements were in preparation for what was confidently expected to be a cavalry breakthrough. It never came off. The days of the cavalry were over and they were no more use in this war than they had been in any war for the previous two hundred years.

After 'B' flights' tour of duty at Auxi-le-Château we returned to Le Crotoy. We did not have very much to do and I am afraid we spent the evening in gambling. I had never gambled before but if you wanted to play cards you had to play for money. I had watched the poker fans very closely for some time and had learnt many of their techniques. This proved very useful when I eventually joined the poker school. I found it very exciting. We played until 2 o'clock in the morning and I seemed to win most evenings. In fact for 3 months I kept myself on my winnings. But I am afraid that some of the chaps played to retrieve their losses because they had no money and expected to be allowed to play on tick.

I have never played poker since. I had in fact found it so exhilarating that I thought it best to make a firm resolve never to play again. When I finally left the Squadron I was owed quite a sum of money which I never got. One officer asked me to take his revolver in part settlement of his debt. I did take it but after the war my Mother was scared stiff at the sight of this weapon in the drawer of my desk at home. It was not loaded of course, but to satisfy her I took all the ammunition down to the river Mersey and threw it in. But to finish the story. Some time in 1919 an order was issued that all arms must be registered. By this time I had left home and returned to London and my Father duly took the revolver to the police-station for registration. But the Police told him that it was Government property having the usual arrows stamped on it, and thereupon confiscated it.

Our tour of duty returned again but it did not last long for me because I went down with influenza and was taken off to a hospital in Abbeville. It was the time of the great 'flu epidemic of 1918. I suppose I was there for about a week. The hospital was very full but every day newcomers from our Squadron kept arriving. If I remember rightly about two-thirds of the officers were stricken and the Squadron was, in effect, out of action.

I then returned to Le Crotoy and my billet. But I did not feel at all well. After a while I was examined by a doctor to see if I was fit for flying again. He reported me unfit for service and certified that I was suffering from 'flying sickness'. This was a new complaint to me but I discovered later that what it really meant was 'war fatigue'. I had been in France for nine months which was very much longer than the usual period of three months for flying officers.

I knew of two other members of our Squadron who, before being sent back to England must have suffered a much worse condition of the same complaint. They had both had long service with the infantry before transferring to the Flying Corps. The first was an observer who could not face crossing the line on his first photographic mission. He took his auxiliary joystick (a thick piece of wood about 18 inches long) and rapped the pilot on the head until he returned home. The other was a pilot who was always unable to fulfil a mission and certainly never crossed the line He always claimed that his engine would not develop sufficient power to climb to the height where he was to rendezvous with the other members of the formation, or that his engine started spluttering or losing revolutions so that he was compelled to return to base. We suspected there was something wrong with him because nothing amiss could ever be found with his engine.

As a result of the doctor's report I was taken to the Duchess of Westminster's Hospital at Le Touquet – a fashionable seaside resort in pre-War days. This was the place where all disabled officers hoped to be taken because it was very luxuriously furnished. I only stayed for two nights and was then hurried off to a hospital (Hôtel Splendide) in Boulogne. After two nights there I went by hospital ship to (I think) Dover. Of course Folkestone was the usual port of arrival from Boulogne, but I am certain that we went to Dover because the hospital train spent the rest of the day and all night wandering around Kent and dropping patients off at various places. I was not told where I was being taken to. I ended up by walking from the train in Charing Cross Station, London, to an ambulance in the station yard. I remember feeling embarrassed at the cheers and flowers that were thrown at the ambulance as we left the station. I felt I was not qualified to be treated as a wounded soldier. The ambulance took me to the London Hospital in Whitechapel Road where, after two days I was sent home on a month's leave.

In concluding this account of my life in the Royal Flying Corps I should like to pay a tribute to the men who served us so well. We knew that our lives were entirely dependent on them doing their job thoroughly. They knew this too and it was this thought that inspired them to give of their best. Apart from the specialists who worked on photography, intelligence, gunnery, stores and office records etc., the others were divided into engine mechanics called 'fitters' and 'riggers' who attended to the rigging of the planes. Each plane had one fitter and one rigger to look after it. As each pilot had his own plane we got to know our own fitters and riggers very well. Both my fitter named Rugg and my rigger named Stocks were competent men who were devoted to me (at least they always behaved as if they were). Rugg had learnt his trade in private life. Stocks was younger than I. What he had done before enlistment I do not know but he had learnt 'rigging' at a Flying Corps school. He had a rather simple nature but was attached to his job. There was always an understanding that the men who attended to a plane should be prepared to go up on a test flight, but there was no compulsion for them to do so. Rugg jumped at the idea whenever I invited him to come with me. He was just happy to listen to the perfect note of his beloved engine as we flew along. We were very dependent on our revolution counters to indicate whether all was well with the engine. But after some experience we learned to listen to the note of the engine and to recognize a changing note which meant that the number of revolutions per minute was falling. Stocks for a long time would never accept an invitation to fly. The Flight Sergeant asked me not to press him because although he was a good willing lad he was rather nervous. On two flights at the end of November 1917, Sergeant Gardner came with me on one flight and Rugg on the other. This must have impressed Stocks because two days later he came and asked if he could come with me. We took off amidst the cheers of all the other mechanics in 'B' flight who all knew about Stocks' previous reluctance to fly.

The mechanics had a hard life. They lived in rather crowded conditions which were not at all attractive. They paraded at daybreak or earlier because we often went off on a job before the sun had risen. It's an impressive sight to watch from a height of 10,000 feet, the sun rising. Very often the planes returned after being damaged by enemy fire or suffered damage in landing. All damage had to be repaired as soon as possible. Sometimes this meant working late into the night with the help of powerful lights. We tried to help them sometimes when things were bad, at least the pilots in 'B' Flight did. We could not do anything to the engines or the rigging. There was one thing that we could do that required no skill and which was always appreciated. This was to wash the plane down.

Each Flight had, as far as I can recall, two fitter corporals and two rigger corporals. Then came two sergeants and one overall Flight Sergeant. At the top were two sergeant-majors – one disciplinary and the other technical. The technical sergeant-major was in charge of all the trucks, tenders, the C.O.'s car and the mechanical workshops. We did not have much to do with him except when we went to him for advice. I would say he was a very competent engineer. The disciplinary sergeant-major had been in the regular army and was an expert in his job. He had a great bristling red moustache of which he was very proud. He looked a really fierce individual and on parade he could make as much noise as any other sergeant-major. I had many contacts with him and discovered that he was not, at heart, a bully. In fact he was a very kind man and even some of the mechanics who had had dealings with him knew about his generous nature. All the 'other ranks' were his care and he looked after them well, was proud of them, and earned their genuine respect.

One first got to know this sergeant-major when one was orderly officer. This job, when we had a full complement of observers to take their part, came round about every six weeks. It involved sleeping in the squadron office at night to answer the telephone calls (if any), inspecting with the sergeant-major the cook-house, the men's sleeping huts and recreation room. The orderly officer had to be present when the mid-day dinner was being served and to taste it. He had also to pay the men if it was pay-day and finally at the end of the day he had to mount the new night guard of the aerodrome. I don't know whether the other officers got to know the sergeant-major as well as I did. They would have spent most of the day with him, as orderly officer, like I did. There was one thing that I did for him, out of respect. I used to sign the outside of his letters, as passed by censor, without even opening them. Of course we all had to take our share in censoring letters. They were usually put on a table in the mess for attention every afternoon. It was well understood that they all had to be cleared by the early evening.

Royal Air Force – 1918

I enjoyed the month's leave I was given on my return from active service in France. At the end of the period I reported, as instructed, to the Air Board in London. Since the formation of the Royal Air Force on 1st April 1918, the Air Board had probably become the Air Ministry, but I am not certain when the change of name took place. I was at any rate, told by one or the other to proceed to a Training Squadron at Spittlegate near Grantham in Lincolnshire. Here I was to take an instructor's course before embarking on an instructor's job at the same place. I did not get on very well with this instructor of instructors. He expected me to rattle off, word for word, the formalised flying instructions he had just repeated to me over the inter-com (only a hollow rubber tube with no amplification). It was a new idea to me for instructors to learn a lot of patter by heart so that they could repeat it to their pupils. I suppose the idea had some merit in that it ensured that the whole of the necessary groundwork was passed on to every pupil. But it did not seem sufficiently flexible to me. Moreover all the people who taught me to fly except the Frenchmen, certainly covered the ground very well. There is no need to expand on this extraordinary system but I will just quote the first instruction 'When you push the stick forward the nose goes down. When you pull the stick back the nose goes up. Elementary my dear Watson!' When we got out of the plane after the second attempt to get me to repeat his ridiculous patter he got rather cross with me. I said I was slightly deaf and could not hear properly what he was saying. In any case, surely it would be better for me to have a copy of the patter which, on the ground, I could learn in five minutes. I certainly exaggerated my degree of deafness. Moreover the condition was improving and it was entirely due to twelve months' continuous flying. My suggestion for improving his technique of training annoyed him still more and he said I would be sent to France. This riled me because it was no part of his job to decide where I should serve. I told him I had already done nine months' service in France which was more than he had done (in fact I was pretty certain he had never been to France, but thought it safer to say I had done longer service). I said, moreover, that I never wanted to be an instructor and would prefer to be a Ferry Pilot i.e. delivering new machines to squadrons, both in England and France. I do not wish to create the impression that we had a flaming row. In fact our altercation was carried on quite politely. The end result was that he promised to recommend me for a Ferry Pilot. And he did.

In the meantime I had nothing to do at Spittlegate until my transfer came through. I was only given one job during the six weeks I was there. I was appointed as the so-called technical member of a Court of Enquiry into the death of a pupil in an air crash. The President of the Court was a Solicitor and as it was his job to conduct this type of Court, he knew, not only all the law and the necessary procedures, but more of the evidence to look for than I did. Anyway he gave me every chance and encouraged me to form my own opinion, when we went to inspect the wreckage. I don't recall what opinions we expressed in our report. All I remember is that he wrote it and I signed it with him.

At the beginning of November 1918 I was duly appointed to the Ferry Pilots' Pool, which had its headquarters in the Orchard Hotel in Orchard Street just off Oxford Street, London. The life there was a curious one. I was given a bed-room to share with another pilot in one of the hotel rooms. I do not think that I saw him more than once in the whole of the two months I was on this job. After reporting for duty at the Adjutant's Office one was sent off, to collect a plane from the place where it had been assembled, with instructions to take it to some training squadron in England or to a squadron on active service in France. The records show that I picked up planes at Sheffield, Coventry and Manchester and took them to Lympne, Marquise (in France), Hendon and Cambridge.

On returning to the Pool after completing a job one was usually allowed three day's rest before being sent off again. So altogether I slept on my first and last nights in the Pool and five times during the intervals between the jobs I was given. The reason why I did not get more than six jobs during my two months with the Pool was the dreadful weather during this, if not every, English winter. I was often stuck for several days in some spot, and once for over a fortnight, waiting for the weather to improve. Even after getting away the visibility would suddenly become bad and I would have to come down at the nearest aerodrome or land in a field and be put up for a night or two by the farmer on whose property I had landed. The secret was to pick a place with what seemed to be an attractive homestead. One had to be prepared to take planes of different kinds. I flew some R.E.8's of the type I had flown in France but until this time I had never previously flown an Armstrong Whitworth, a D.H.9 or a Bristol Fighter.

It may seem strange but the safety of one article was more important than that of the plane itself. This article was the watch which fitted in the dashboard of the plane. These watches were fairly large pocket watches which kept perfect time. It was everybody's ambition to possess one. The result was that when you took away a new plane you had to sign a receipt for the watch but not for the plane. When you arrived at your destination to deliver the plane you had to produce the watch from your pocket and get a receipt in return. On one occasion I forgot to hand over the watch but honesty compelled me to go back and hand it over to a very grateful stores corporal.

Long distance flights were rather boring in those days, because they took such a long time. There was nothing to do but keep your eye on your map and follow the route you had planned. We depended almost entirely on landmarks to find our way. I can remember only one place where we allowed ourselves to be guided by compass. After crossing the Thames on the east side of London you could steer southeast and forget about landmarks until you recognized an exceptional long straight road which passed through Ashford in Kent.

On these long flights I used to try and keep myself entertained by engaging in races with express trains that were going in my direction. It was only when there was a very strong head wind against me that the competition was anything like a real battle, but it might have been a little more intense if the engine driver had known what was happening.

~

My first job as a Ferry Pilot was, on 4 November 1918, to take an R.E.8 from Coventry to Marquise a few miles northeast of Boulogne. My route lay across the east side of London, but when I reached the Thames I could see a very heavy haze ahead. So I turned back hoping to land at Hendon (just north of London). On my way I suddenly found myself in heavy cloud above an aerodrome which I thought was Hendon. After landing and getting my plane attended to I enquired how I could get to London where I proposed to spend the night. I was told that I could pick up a bus outside the 'Bell Inn' a little way down a lane. This I did but the journey to London insteading of taking half an hour through suburbs, as I had expected it would from the 'Bell', Hendon (of which I had heard) went on for nearly an hour through open country. I therefore asked a surprised bus conductor where I had got on the bus. He told me it was London Colney, which I knew was between St Albans and Watford. Very shortly after my enquiry the bus passed through the suburbs of London which I recognized. In bed that night I could not help thinking what an extraordinary thing it was that the place where I actually landed had a pub of the same unusual name as that at the place where I thought I had landed. I also wondered what would have happened if I had had to tell the authorities at the Pilots' Pool that on my return to Hendon to collect my plane I had been unable to find it.

The next morning I left the Pilots' Pool where I had been sleeping and returned by bus to London Colney. I picked up my plane and flew to Hendon where I landed because the weather had become rather threatening. I got away after a short stay and then, when I had got as far as the English Channel I again found the weather too bad for flying. I turned back once more and landed at Lympne in Kent. I had passed over this aerodrome on my way to the coast. The weather must have been pretty bad because I see from my log book that I stayed for two nights at Lympne before crossing the Channel to Marquise. It was the first time I had flown over the English Channel and I remember flying at a very low height from ship to ship (in case of engine failure) taking care not to cross the French coast east of Cap Gris Nez where some unfortunates had landed in territory occupied by the Germans.

My next job was on 10 November 1918, when I was sent to Sheffield to pick up another R.E.8 which had to be taken to Lympne. But I only got as far as Harlaxton aerodrome near Grantham in Lincolnshire where the bad weather forced me to spend the night. It seemed better in the morning so I got off fairly early. The day was 11th November and before leaving I had learnt that an Armistice was to be signed with the Germans that day. Anyway by the time I had got as far as Huntingdon the weather had once again taken an ominous turn so I decided to turn back and land at an aerodrome at Stamford in Lincolnshire. I remember saying to myself 'I don't want to be killed on the day the war ends'. On landing I asked about Flight Lieutenant Hedley who had served with me in No.6 Squadron in France. I knew that he had been posted to Stamford as an instructor. He was quickly found and, after greeting me he took me to his rented house where he was living with his wife. We had a very pleasant evening and dinner. We did go for a short stroll after dinner to see what was happening in the town. There were a few people out in the streets celebrating the Armistice but it was all very decorous and nothing like the riotous behaviour I found in London the following evening. When we got back to his house Hedley took me round to the house next door where he had arranged for me to sleep.

I should record here that Hedley was an English engineer who had been trained at Vickers and had emigrated to Australia in 1910. He served with the Australian Forces for three years and then transferred to the Royal Flying Corps. When I arrived in Australia the Hedleys were the only people I knew and I subsequently tell how I caught up with them again in December 1938 – twenty years later.

I only stayed the one night in Stamford. I got away in the morning and much to my delight, made my way to Lympne without meeting with any of the usual bad weather. I was, of course, anxious to get back to London and to join in the Armistice celebrations. So I caught the first available train and was in London by the mid-afternoon. Even at this time the streets were full of shouting and singing revellers. In Trafalgar Square I saw Australian soldiers lighting a fire at the foot of Nelson's Column. The plinth was badly damaged and the marks of the fire can still be seen. By seven o'clock or so it was impossible to walk in comfort along any street in the West End. But no-one wanted to do so. Everybody wanted to be in at the fun. Great circles were formed by people holding hands and revolving around. In other places mobs of irresponsible youths were dashing in mass formation into the crowds. Mostly it was good natured fun but I am afraid that many young girls relaxed their usual moral standards in the streets of London that night. I eventually got back to bed in the Pilots' Pool about 2 a.m. but it did not matter because I knew there would be no job for me the next day. I stayed in London for four nights before setting forth again. I went out again on the next night but did not stay there very long. I should say that by about the fourth day people were beginning to settle down.

On 16 November 1918 I was sent to Sheffield to collect an Armstrong-Whitworth for delivery to Hendon. After an hour's flying the weather got too bad so I turned back and landed at Upton, near Newark-on-Trent, Nottinghamshire. The next day after 35 minutes flying, I got as far as Grantham where I landed at Spittlegate aerodrome. There was too much heavy cloud and rain about to get away until two days later. Even so I got no further than Stamford where I was forced down by fog. I had to wait at Stamford for a few hours before I could get away and then after becoming boxed in by fog, after an hour's flying, I was forced to land on a farm near Hatfield, Hertforshire. I had picked a very good farmhouse and was made very welcome by the farmer, his wife and a Highland officer in uniform. The farmer, a Scot, seemed to be very prosperous and claimed he was showing the district what Scottish farming methods could do. But what a bully' and how rude he was to his wife who was much younger. At times it was embarrassing to be in a room with them. She obviously turned to the young handsome Scotsman for comfort and support. He had been blinded in one eye during the war and was recuperating on the farm partly with a view to becoming a farmer himself. From various little incidents that I observed I began to suspect that he was the wife's lover. After staying with these people for two nights it looked as though I might be able to get away. I therefore organized the farmer to bring some of his labourers along to hold on to the plane while the young Scotsman sat in the pilot's seat and I swung the propeller to start the engine.

I had explained to the young Scotsman that all he had to do was to hold the joy-stick to his stomach to prevent the plane tippling over on its nose when the engine started and that, as the throttle was fully open, he should pull it right back to slow running as soon as the engine started. Everything went off to perfection and we were now ready for off. I say 'we' because the young Scotsman had asked if he could come with me to Hendon. It was against all the rules and regulations to take unofficial passengers but as he was at any rate wearing a uniform I chanced it. But the weather became terrible and after flying for thirty-five minutes I dropped in to London Colney again. We both got on the bus at the 'Bell Inn' and journeyed to London. I was not worried about the length of the journey this time.

We had dinner together in Soho in the evening. The fog around London was very bad and it was not until six days later that I went off to London Colney to collect my plane and deliver it to Hendon as instructed eleven days previously.

On 3 December 1918 I was 'sent to Coventry' to collect another R.E.8. I have no idea where I was supposed to take it to because I never got there. I got away all right but not for long. After an hour I had to land at Castle Bromwich, near Birmingham, because of the usual fog. Here I stayed for four days during which I recall going to a theatre in Birmingham one night and another rather riotous night until the early hours of the morning in the pilots' mess. I got aloft two days after my arrival but only for fifteen minutes in what is recorded as a test flight. When I eventually started on my journey I had to descend near Wolverhampton, again because of fog. I landed in a field and was put up by a farmer and his wife. They were a nice but simple couple and not so prosperous as the couple I had stayed with at Hatfield. In the morning of the next day I was invited to visit the wife of the local squire. Sherry was provided on arrival and later a very pleasant lunch.

By the way, I am still puzzled as to where I was making for. Coventry, Castle Bromwich and Wolverhampton are in a line running north west but all my other journeys were in a southerly direction.

Two days after my arrival at farm, the weather looked a little more promising for getting away. My problem, though, as usual was the arrangements to be made for the take-off. I had a number of farm hands around me but not one of them was willing to sit in the cockpit while I swung the propeller. I therefore got four men to hold the two wings and another two men to hold down the tail plane. I warned them all beforehand that there would be a terrific blast of air when the engine started but that they must hold on at all costs. I then put the throttle in the fully-open position and got ready to swing the propeller. For some unknown reason the engine actually started on the first swing and I dashed around to climb into the cockpit and pull back the throttle. But courage failed the four men at the front when the plane moved a little bit and when they let go the machine started to move forward in a wide circle at gradually increasing speed and dragging the two valiant men at the rear still hanging on like grim death. By this time I had got round to the side of the machine near the pilot's seat and was running at full speed trying to reach the switch on the outside of the plane. My fingers almost touched the switch (much the same as a light switch) but I was beaten off by the increasing speed at which the plane was tearing along. The two men at the rear were eventually forced to let go and as I gave up the chase the plane turned up on its nose, smashed the propeller and damaged the wings. My next job was to phone the aerodrome at Castle Bromwich to ask them to send a gang to take the plane away. They sent two men immediately to guard the plane. They were rather elderly men and they arrived with their blankets, with which to sleep under the wings or in the cockpit, but without food or money. So I went along to the local pub whose landlord agreed to provide them with a good hot dinner, for which I paid. When they went off to dinner I stayed and guarded the plane. They returned very pleased with their outing especially as they had been provided with a good supply of beer at my expense. I later went back to the farm house to sleep and left the next morning after the repair gang had arrived with a lorry to take the plane away.

Early in December 1918 I went to Manchester to collect a D.H.9 which I had to take to Cambridge. The weather was so dreadful that I must have lived at home (18 miles from Manchester) for nearly three weeks. I phoned the Manchester aerodrome every morning to see if there was any chance of getting away. As a result of this delay I was able to spend Christmas at home.

I had not previously flown a D.H.9 so on 30 December 1918 I took one up for twenty-five minutes on a test flight. This plane was fitted with a new and very powerful American 'Liberty Engine'. It was a little disconcerting on climbing into the cockpit to read a notice in front of the pilot's seat saying 'On no account open this engine beyond [a certain number of] revolutions per minute'.

When I reached this number (I don't remember what it was) there still seemed to be a lot of reserve power in the engine. I had planned the route I would take to get to Cambridge and gathered the appropriate maps. First of all, though, I was to make for my home at Warrington. From there I was to follow the railway line to Stafford and then strike in a south easterly direction for Cambridge. When I arrived over my home in Warrington my parents, in whose house I had slept the previous night, were ready for me and my Father was out in the garden waving a large sheet. After I had circled around the house three times at about 300 feet the engine made an ominous report like a backfire and emitted a puff of black smoke. So I immediately made for the open country. Fortunately nothing further eventuated but I was somewhat amused when my Father, two days later, said 'We got the message when you were about to leave'.

As everything seemed to be all right I continued on my way to Stafford. Here I turned to the east and found myself over an absolute network of railway lines which I could not distinguish on my map. To make matters worse the appropriate map then blew overboard. I knew I was over Cannock Chase but that was not much help.

I also knew I had to fly in a south easterly direction and this I proceeded to do in the hope of sighting an aerodrome or some landmark I could recognize.

I don't know how long I flew without getting any satisfactory results but I eventually decided to land and ask somebody where I was. I therefore picked out a field in which to land. I have already said that I had not flown a D.H.9 before but when I attempted to land the thing would not stop running along the ground and continuing to charge towards the distant boundary. So up I went. If it had been the R.E.8 I had flown in France I could have put it down into any old corner of a small field.

I therefore tried to land in larger fields but when I got down there I found I could not avoid the cattle. So up I went again.

It's an awful feeling to be unable to land when you want, because you know you will have to come down sometime. Anyway I carried on in a south easterly direction. I then decided to try to read the names on the platforms of railway stations. The ones I could read were isolated country stations which I could not find on my map (I had already moved out of the area for which I had lost my map). I then went down over the station of a fairly large town but because chimneys were nearby I could not get low enough to read the name. (Incidentally, when returning to Manchester by train two days later I recognised this unknown station as we passed through. It was Wellingborough.)

The only thing I could do was to continue my lonely journey. How relieved I was when I suddenly spotted an aerodrome below. It was Stamford which was only 35 miles from Cambridge. Anyway I had had enough excitement for a while so I landed to ask for petrol. Only an excuse really – what I wanted was a rest after my day's adventures. I took off eventually, little knowing that I was in for still further adventures. It must have been fairly late when I left Stamford because it was quite dark when I arrived over the Cambridge aerodrome. Anyway here I was at last at my destination so I glided down. As I came in to land I misjudged my height in the dark and hit the ground a terrific whack. The result of this was that the plane bounced thirty feet or more into the air because I vividly remember seeing the hangers some distance below when I was at the top of the bounce. I was in a difficult situation. What is more, and it is something I have not mentioned, I knew I was to be demobilized the next day – 'What a day to crash!', I remember saying at the top of that bounce, and 'Christ, I will never fly again'. It was not blasphemy, it was a solemn oath. The real danger I was in was that if I stuck my nose down and again tried to land I would probably stall and crash to the ground. This had been the cause of many fatal accidents. Fortunately I was a fairly experienced pilot by this time, so I gave my engine full throttle at the top of the bounce and sailed around the aerodrome in order to come in to try again to land. This time I was successful. I saw nothing of Cambridge. I made my way by car straight to the railway station where I caught a late train to London and thence to the Ferry Pilots' Headquarters.

Two mornings later I was given the necessary papers and a travel warrant to the Demobilization Centre at Manchester. It was on this journey that I recognized Wellingborough as the place where I had tried to read the name of the station. The demobilization arrangements were well organized and I was soon out of the place and on my way home to Warrington, a civilian once again though still in officer's uniform. Altogether I had flown 327 hours of which 236 hours had been on active service in France.

I know even now that I was more than glad to be out – I was relieved. One knew quite well that the survival rate of pilots was low. But at the start when one was young one did not worry about such things. Basically I think one thought 'it could not happen to me'. But after nearly two years in which one was constantly losing one's comrades, one realized that there was only one inevitable end. Years later I read a book *Winged Victory* by V.M. Yeates who, in spite of his courage and resolution, hints at the same underlying demoralization that eventually set in.

People often express surprise to me that anyone would have been willing to fly the machines which we operated during the 1914–18 War. They are comparing our fragile craft with the modern aeroplane. But we compared our planes with those which had been in existence before the War. We thought ours were marvellous in comparison.

During the Second World War I was often amazed at the courage and fortitude which men could display in appalling circumstances. You would not think any human being could stand such strains. People have said similar things to me about life in the Royal Flying Corps during the First War. What helped my generation was our youth, a time when risks hold no terrors, and the mental as well as the physical discipline which was instilled into us. We were discouraged from taking unnecessary risks. There were times when a job had to be done regardless of the risks. In our Squadron the ones who took unnecessary risks, without orders, like straffing enemy observation balloons in the unsuitable machines which we flew, may have been hoping for a medal (though some of them never learnt how to measure risks) but in the end they lost their lives.

Government Actuary's Department – 1919–38

I was demobilized in early January 1919 nearly two months after Armistice Day. I was lucky to get out so quickly – entirely because the War Office applied for my release. I had a month's holiday at home and then, at the beginning of February returned to London to start work again in the same branch of the War Office where I had been before enlistment. I think I was the first ex-serviceman to return. Thereafter, every few days, one or other of my old colleagues drifted back. At the start I went to live with my Uncle and Aunt at Golders Green, but after Easter I joined my school friend Harold Emmerson in the digs at Brondesbury where we had been living before I enlisted.

Shortly after I had settled down the Civil Service Commission announced two entry examinations for returned soldiers. The first was for the First Division, the top grade in the Service while the other was for the Intermediate Division, between the First Division and the Second Division, to which I had been appointed in 1914. I stood no chance of getting a place in the First Division but Harold Emmerson, who was serving in the Intermediate Division did, because of his record in winning the Warrington University scholarship and an exhibition at the South Kensington Imperial College of Science. He sat and was successful.

I did decide to sit for the Intermediate examination from which appointments would be made to certain specialized Departments such as Inland Revenue, Exchequer and Audit and the Government Actuary's. The last named Department appealed to me. The requirements were that candidates should be under age 24 and have remained at school until the age of 18. These conditions applied to everybody who wanted to sit for the examination but those who fancied the Government Actuary's Department were required to pass a later examination in mathematics. In addition they were offered a salary rise to £200 p.a. on passing Part II of the examination of the Institute of Actuaries. I suppose the possibility of extra remuneration was quite acceptable to me but the main attraction was the mathematical basis of actuarial work. Mathematics had been the only subject in which I had distinguished myself at school. As it was nearly five years since I had left school this meant a lot of work to rub up my mathematics. There was no need for special study for the main examination because the subjects were based mainly on general knowledge and English expression. The main examination was to be held in May and any successful candidate could then sit for the mathematics examination in July.

The idea of having to study for at least four years after entry into the Civil Service was a new idea. It is probably more common nowadays (it certainly is in Australia) but in England at that time it was enough to put many people off. I remember that my Aunt with whom I was living at the time, and whose husband was a Civil Servant, suggested I was foolish to commit myself to all this work. But I had other ideas. I thought that with professional qualifications the avenues for employment would be widened.

Anyway, I did work hard, sat for and passed both examinations. I think I was 41st out of 50 successful candidates in the main examination, and 8th out of 8 successful in the maths exam. I was disappointed with the results in mathematics but I have a clear recollection of mucking up two out of fifteen or so questions set in the two papers.

Anyway I had achieved my objective and I started work in the Government Actuary's Department on 1st September 1919.

The Government Actuary's Department had been started (though under a different name) as a result of the National Insurance Act of 1911. The new Act provided for the payment of a cash benefit during sickness and the granting of medical benefit to employees whose earnings were less than £400 p.a. The scheme was financed by the contributions of workers and their employers together with a Government subsidy. The Bill had met with a stormy reception during its passage through Parliament and there had been subsequent troubles in getting the doctors to play their part in the administration. The resolute action of the Government caused the doctors' revolt to collapse as soon as the scheme came into operation. Anyway the scheme had got well on the way by 1914 but the 1914 – 18 War had impeded any further development. The day to day work was performed by about two thousand non-profit organizations subject to Government approval, direction and supervision. Each Approved Society and indeed each of those which were branches of a large organization like the Manchester Unity of Oddfellows, were financially independent though protected by a series of contingencies funds. The Department, when I arrived, was just starting to value by actuarial methods each of these two thousand Approved Societies. As can be imagined it was a very large task. There is no point in going into the technicalities of the operation. I knew nothing at all about them myself when I started work. My job and that of my other junior colleagues was to multiply various numbers together on a machine, add or subtract them and by some magical process to determine whether each society had a surplus or a deficiency. As a brief explanation I might say that a surplus arose when the value of the invested securities plus the discounted value of contributions which the members would pay in the future were greater than the discounted value of the benefits they could be expected to receive in the future.

There is no disguising the fact that the work was extremely monotonous and boring and continued to be so for some years until I had passed some of the examinations of the Institute of Actuaries and learnt what all the calculations really amounted to. The Government Actuary was Sir Alfred Watson who, during the debates in Parliament on the National Insurance Bill had been the actuarial adviser to the Opposition. He had done this with such distinction, as compared with the Government's own actuarial advisers, that Lloyd George invited him to join the National Insurance Commission. This led later to his enlarged appointment as Government Actuary. There had not been a Government Actuary for nearly seventy years. John Finlaisen who was Government Actuary from 1822–1851 was also the first President of the Institute of Actuaries 1848–60. He had qualified for the Scottish Bar and on visiting London in 1804 secured a job in the Admiralty by political influence – the usual method at the time. Thereafter his career throws an interesting light on the history of England in the first half of the last century. His principal efforts on behalf of the British Government were:

(1) Reorganization of Admiralty records which were in a chaotic state since nothing had been done with them since Pepys, who in 1684 became Secretary to the Admiralty, wrote a memorandum on the subject.

(2) To advise on several pension funds for civil employees of the Admiralty.

(3) To advise the Treasury on financial matters and to become the Government Actuary in charge of the National Debt Office.

(4) As a result of the abolition of slavery he was called upon to calculate the compensation to be paid to the slave owners. His estimate of £15,000,000 was adopted and paid.

(5) To be closely associated with the Act of 1847 providing for the compulsory registration of births, deaths and marriages.

(6) Finally, he protested in vain to the Treasury that the annuities which were being sold by the National Debt Office as a method of helping to pay for the War of American Independence were actually a source of loss to the Exchequer instead of profit.

Apart from the valuation of Approved Societies (already referred to), the Government Actuary's Department from 1919 onwards carried out a number of actuarial investigations into pension funds and reported upon existing and projected Social Security legislation. It examined and reported to the Board of Trade upon the annual returns of Life Insurance Companies. It prepared life tables from the results of the 1921 and subsequent censuses. It published a very valuable book which was in effect a detailed guide to all Government statistical publications. We were in fact the actuarial advisers to the Treasury and any other Departments in need of assistance. The Treasury turned to us for advice on loan flotation's and the National Insurance Commission depended largely on us for financial guidance.

So although I said a little way back that the work was terribly dull at the start, it gradually became very interesting. It might not have suited everybody but it did me. This was because of the mathematical basis behind most of the work.

My real development as an actuary started in 1926 when the Government appointed a Royal Commission to report upon National Insurance. The Government Actuary, Sir Alfred Watson was a member of this Royal Commission and also the Chairman of its Actuarial Advisory Committee which included two consulting actuaries in private practice. The Secretary to the Committee was Maurice Knowles and I was his assistant. Between us we did all the investigations and performed all the involved calculations that we hoped would help the Committee. This was a happy association with Maurice. Thereafter we were closely associated in the work on National Insurance for several years. He then moved on to other work while I took his place as the expert on National Insurance. We lunched together nearly every day for many years. Our families had a holiday together at Woolacombe in Devon in 1936. They saw us off when we left for Australia in 1938. He came to Australia on an official job in 1950 and we have always spent some time with him on our various trips back to England. Needless to say we have maintained a fairly regular correspondence for nearly 40 years.

When I was first appointed to the Government Actuary's Department my title was Actuarial Assistant. After passing the Institute of Actuaries examinations we were qualified for promotion to the rank of Assistant Actuary, then Actuary, then Principal Actuary and then for a few and with luck to Deputy Government Actuary or even Government Actuary. I was promoted to Assistant Actuary in 1933. It had been a wait of fourteen years – much too long in fact. It was a pity it had to be so. It resulted in some people losing their enthusiasm. But I can honestly say that I never did. Nevertheless the quite substantial increase in salary to £850 p.a. was very welcome. It seems an insignificant amount today. But it was quite good money in 1933. From all the immediate post-war entrants to the Department (about thirty) I was the second to be promoted. Although I ought to be more modest, I must say that the first promotee was the best and I believe that I was the second best of the whole bunch.

I well remember the day on which I received my promotion. I was sharing a large room with two colleagues at the time when the Staff Clerk (a non-professional officer) came in and whispered to me that the 'Chief' (i.e. the Government Actuary) was going to send for me and tell me of my promotion. I make no comment on the rights and wrongs of his action but I still think it was intended as a kindly act. I know it re-enforced me for the coming interview because we juniors did not have much contact with the 'Chief'. In fact I had never engaged in conversation with him and had done nothing more than pass the time of day with him in the corridor. Anyway about five minutes later my telephone rang and the G.A.'s secretary told me that the 'Chief' wanted to see me. The interview went off very well and I was duly informed of what was to happen. Afterwards the Deputy Government Actuary told me that the 'Chief' was very impressed when I said that I had always been deeply interested in National Insurance. Although the remark was not made with any ulterior motive at all, I realized afterwards why it was a most fortunate one. Before his appointment as Government Actuary Sir Alfred had been the Actuary to the Manchester Unity from about the age of 23 so that Friendly Societies and our Approved Societies had been his life interest.

I saw more of Sir Alfred after my promotion but I remember most of all one particular incident which happened about three years later. At this time he was about 65 and unfortunately his mental capacity had declined very rapidly. He had been an undoubted genius until then and to see this deterioration was sad. Occasionally a number of letters got to him direct and he had developed a practice of dictating a reply on the spot and sending off the letter. His personal typist had therefore been instructed to show all such letters to various officers who were knowledgeable about certain aspects of the work. She was instructed to show me all his letters dealing with National Insurance. One day she brought a letter to me which was hopelessly off the beam. I took it round to the person next in rank to the Deputy Government

Actuary Mr Epps, who was away on leave. This person did not know as much about the subject matter as I did but after I had explained it to him he said he would tackle Watson. Well! about ten minutes later I got a ring telling me to go and see the 'Chief'. He would normally have called me 'Balmford' but I knew I was in the dog-house when he said 'Mister Balmford' very slowly and deliberately, 'You seem to have found something wrong with this letter of mine'. I tried to explain (in fact I still believe that I did succeed in doing so quite well) what was wrong with the letter. But no, he would not listen to me and waving his arm for me to get out, dismissed me. I walked away and when I had the door half open I turned round and said 'Sir Alfred, I beg you not to sign that letter until you have shown it to Mr Epps'. I heard nothing more until Mr Epps, on his return from leave, rang and said 'Balmford, Thank you for stopping that letter'. I must have impressed the 'Chief' more than he revealed to me. I never saw him again. He died shortly afterwards.

London – 1919–38

After living with Auntie Lizzie and Uncle Joseph for three months after my taking up work again at the War Office I went back to the digs in Brondesbury where I had been living before joining the Army. The landlady was Mrs Diethelm with her daughter Isobel. The mother was a Scotswoman of over 70 who had married a Swiss. The daughter in her late forties had a strong German accent. Even at her advanced age and after living in Switzerland for many years Mrs Diethelm had retained a strong Scotch accent.

I shared a sitting room and bed-room once again with my old school friend Harold Emmerson. It has been a long and happy association with Harold from our schooldays until today. We had many arguments but I can't remember that we ever quarrelled. The other occupants of the House were Miss Tomeer, a middle-aged Dutch spinster who was employed as a translator by some firm. Two other fellows shared another bed-room and sitting room. One, Aychbourne, was a professional violinist who had just qualified at the London Academy of Music. His friend 'Dusty Miller' was a chauffeur to a prominent knight who had been (I think) Chief Commissioner of the Metropolitan Police Force.

Miss Tomeer amused Harold and me because although her innards were making constant gurgling noises she could sit throughout a meal as though nothing was happening. Dusty Miller is remembered for his vamping on a grand piano which he owned and his worries about the constancy of the girl with whom he was in love. I attended a coming out performance which Aychbourne gave at the Queens Hall with a full orchestral accompaniment. I don't know who paid for the expenses but from the way he lived he must have had some financial backer. I at any rate reduced the losses because I insisted on paying for two tickets although I had been offered a free one. Val came with me. Neither Harold nor I had any social contacts with these boarders, other than at meal times.

It was during the last three months of 1919 that I was studying hard for Part I of the Institute of Actuaries examinations. I usually had dinner in the digs or sometimes with Harold and F.E. Norman at Flemings in Oxford Street. Norman was much older than Harold and I but still a bachelor. He had an innocent eye for the girls and christened our waitress 'Bright Eyes'. I was usually back in the digs soon after seven o'clock when I proceeded to get down to the revision of my mathematics until ten o'clock or so. After that Harold and I frequently had a game of 'Rummy' to take my mind off my work. This procedure was carried on in later years.

My relationships with Val (who subsequently became my wife) were somewhat intermittent during 1919. I had first taken her out to dinner in February 1917 just before joining the Artists' Rifles. Throughout the war she worked in the same branch of the War Office where I had been employed. She was appointed a Junior Administration Assistant. As such her basic salary was greater than mine. But having been classified as Administrative she was not paid overtime, whereas I more than doubled my basic salary with overtime. We corresponded occasionally when I was in the Forces and met whenever I was on leave in London. But the real development in our relationship occurred during the 1919 August Bank Holiday, when Harold and I joined Val and her sister Hilda for the weekend during their holiday at Folkestone.

My meetings with Val then became more regular, usually one evening during the week and on either Saturday or Sunday. Sometimes we went to a show; in summer we might sit in and wander around Hyde Park; in winter we frequently walked to West Norwood where she lived. This meant a fairly long bus ride home for me because I was living on the other side of London at Brondesbury. I had to change buses at Victoria and I usually slipped into a delicatessen which provided very good sandwiches. This arrangement continued until Christmas 1920 when I took Val home to Warrington for the first time. We became engaged shortly after our return to London. In August

1921 she came with me to join, at Cadgwith in Cornwall, my Father, Mother, Ruth, Olive and friends of Ruth's. It was on this holiday that we sailed to the Scilly Isles. Val who had always fancied herself as a good sailor, though she had done nothing more than potter around in some bay or other, discovered something of the distress that can arise at sea.

The experience was repeated in 1922, when after our wedding on 20th June we sailed from Southampton to Guernsey on our honeymoon. Actually the sea was perfectly calm, so there was no excuse for being sick except perhaps because we shared a very small and stuffy cabin. On the whole it was not a very good start to a honeymoon. We had gone to Guernsey for three weeks. We explored the less interesting half of the island during the first week when Val was not at her best as a result of the voyage, and we intended, when she was better, to do the rest of the island. My recollection is that Guernsey had a very beautiful coast line but that the interior was mainly covered with greenhouses used for forcing tomatoes, vegetables and flowers for the English market. Anyway, when the second week started the rain also started. And did it rain! It poured for a whole week so we cleared out and returned to London after a fortnight. It must have been bad for anyone to break off a honeymoon. Moreover we both realized that we could be better employed at home getting the new house (32 Elwood Avenue, Kenton, near Harrow) into ship shape.

On the return journey to Falmouth Val was very sick again. But there was plenty of excuse this time. The passage was very rough with mountainous seas and heavy rain. There was no cabin to be had, so I put Val on a sort of bunk at the side of the main saloon. I could not stay there, because I knew I would be sick. So I tipped a steward to look after her and dashed down every so often to see how she was. I spent my time alone on the deck (all the other passengers seemed to be sick). I knew that if I stayed up there I would be all right in the fresh air.

When we got back to Kenton we found (as expected) that the furniture had been moved in and the next morning we started to straighten up the place and so commenced our married life. The first baby (named Peter) arrived on 10th May 1924. There had been a sudden influx of cases into the Maternity Home so Val had to return home sooner than expected. After I had brought her back in a taxi we settled in the dining room – I in one armchair and she in another with the new baby on her lap. Neither of us had had any experience of infants, and we just did not know what to do next. I remember saying 'Do you think I could smoke?' I got permission and I had no sooner lit my cigarette than the baby piddled right across the carpet. This was a highly intelligent manoeuvre by Peter (as he was afterwards called) because it showed us what we had to do, namely change the napkin, and mop up the mess on the floor. For the next 20 years we were never again at a loss what to do with him.

The next baby (named John David but, because of Peter, called Paul for a few days) arrived on 4th March 1931. On this occasion I was in the Westminster Baths during my lunchtime when the Superintendent came in, blew a whistle and said 'Anybody here named Balmford'. I did not need to ask what I was wanted for because the midwife had settled in the house a day or so previously. Someone had evidently phoned the office from home and the message had then been passed on to the Baths. Anyway I got home as quickly as I could but there was nothing doing until much later in the day. So I had to go through the agony of sitting around, calling the doctor and waiting anxiously while he was upstairs, and finally being relieved when I was told that it was a boy. I was then allowed to go and inspect him and his mother.

Although Peter was around at the time, he had gone to bed before the doctor had arrived. He had previously been told what was to happen but whether he knew the event was imminent I do not recall. Anyway he was anxious to see the baby when I told him the next morning. He then started to ask a lot of questions, which I did my best to answer frankly. Later in the day I got a book called, I think, *The Cradle Story*, which he proceeded to study and to learn some of the facts of life. The book was not in the modern style being based on the birds and the bees.

One of the surprises I got after John arrived was to find that he was quite different from Peter. I sort of thought that the second child would be a repeat (excuse the pun) of the first. But I was quickly disillusioned when John's personality began to develop. Peter was always very proud of John and was very good and kind to him. John's respect for his elder brother only lessened when he himself reached the age of twelve or so.

Top

Walter's sons Peter and John at Birchington, England, 1934.

Bottom

Peter and John, in the garden in Canberra in 1948.

Top

Peter Balmford (1924–2005) in Greenland, 2003.

Bottom

John David Balmford (b.1931).

There is not much more of importance to say about the life in London until 1938. Because of lack of funds most of our holidays in the early years were spent in Warrington where we went to stay with my parents in summer and also at Christmas. They also visited us twice a year. Later on we managed to afford holidays at such places as Swanage, Llandudno, Birching ten and Woolacombe. Peter went to school at 'Alpha' in Harrow, and then to Merchant Taylors at Rickmansworth. John went to a preparatory school called Quainton Hall. He did not go to Alpha because I felt that Peter had been rather neglected during his last year when he was studying for a scholarship to Merchant Taylors. He did not win a scholarship because the extra tuition which had been promised did not materialize. I still think he would otherwise have been successful.

As I have said more about Peter than about John I will just record a few things about John.

He was a bit slow about beginning to 'sit up' and later on 'to walk'. I remember having him on my knees in a sitting position but supporting his back. If I removed my hand he would immediately drop into a lying position. Neither Val nor I ever tried to force the boys to do these things but John showed no interest in sitting for quite a while after he ought to have been doing so. He did not walk until he was 17 months old and that was when we were on holiday at Llandulno.

Another story about John concerns an incident at a school concert. He had been chosen to recite a short, poem

The stout brown trout swam in and out
That's all I know about the stout brown trout.

Before John's effort there had been some slapstick performance in which boiled rice had been thrown around. Unfortunately, it had not all been swept up so that when John arrived in the centre of the stage he slipped on the rice. He put on a very good performance, kept his balance and what is more, recited his short piece to perfection. It brought the house down.

In England, whenever a new king succeeds to the throne, the fact is formally announced by a Herald who reads the Proclamation. He is all dressed up in his uniform and rides on horseback to various locations. The first location is at the foot of Charles I's statue in Trafalgar Square. The next is at the entrance to the City of London and the final one, I think, at the Mansion House. After the abdication of Edward VIII I happened to be in Trafalgar Square with John when along came the Herald to proclaim the accession of George VI. So we stood right beside him while he did his stuff. Before the Herald started I told John (aged five) that he should try to remember seeing this ceremony because he would probably never see another. But today he remembers nothing about it.

I don't think I will rack my brains anymore in an endeavour to think of any/further incidents during this period but I just want to put on record my results in the Institute of Actuaries Examinations.

		Date of Exam.		Result
Part IA	Mathematics	Nov.	1919	Passed
Part IB	Theory of Interest	Nov.	1919	Passed
Part II	Life Contingencies	May	1920	Failed
		Nov.	1920	Failed
		May	1921	Passed
Part IIIA	Construction and	May	1922	Failed
	Graduation of Tables	May	1923	Passed
Part IIIB	Life Office Work	May	1923	Passed
Part IV	More advanced stages of IIIB plus Friendly Societies, Pension Funds and Law	May	1924	Did not sit
		May	1925	Did not sit
		May	1926	Failed
		May	1927	Passed

It is interesting to recall that Parts IB and IIIB which I passed at first try, were the ones I knew least about. I passed because I tackled questions from first principles.

My poorest exhibitions were in Parts II and IV. It is rather strange. In Part II I had thoroughly mastered the subject and had been top in all the pre-examination tests. I think I was over-confident.

Part IV reveals a sad story. The examination was to be held in May 1924 and this was the month in which Peter was expected to be born. I realized that I would not be able to do much work during the two months before his arrival, so I stopped all further study in March and did not enter for the examination. I think I had a good knowledge of my subject by May 1925 but unfortunately on the morning of the examination I felt like nothing on earth. So I went round to see the Doctor. I asked him if he could give me something to freshen me up and keep me going throughout the examination. He replied that he could give me something which would make me feel better for a few hours but that I would afterwards feel worse than ever. He said I had influenza and the best thing I could do was to go back to bed, which I did. He kept me in bed for a fortnight before letting me get up.

In 1926 I was still better equipped but the examination was held in the middle of the famous General Strike. As a result there were only occasional trains running to the city from Kenton, where we lived. I therefore stayed for three nights at the Euston Hotel in London in order to get to the examination centre. This upset was the main cause of my failure. When I sat again in May 1927 I was more worried than I had ever been prior to an examination. I knew my subject perfectly but after studying the same subjects for four years I was feeling stale. When the examination was over I knew I had not done as well as I ought to have done but they let me through. Afterwards I became an Assistant Examiner for two years and then a member of the Examination Board for another two years.

I now come to the really crucial change in my life. During 1937 and 1938 Sir Walter Kinnear, who was the head of the National Insurance Division of the Ministry of Health, had been in Australia advising upon the introduction of a scheme of National Insurance. When we saw the report which he submitted we thought it was too much of a scissors and paste rendering of the English scheme without any adaptation for different conditions in Australia. Sir Walter had been asked to ascertain if the Government Actuary's Department could lend an actuary to the Australian Government for three years to help in the introduction of the proposed scheme. Epps, who was now Government Actuary had been told of this and had replied that he did not wish any more people to go away on loan because the Department had already one officer on loan to India and another to New Zealand. He offered however, to ascertain if any qualified officer was willing to move permanently to Australia. This suggestion was accepted by the Australian authorities. Epps told Maurice Knowles and me that the choice should lie between the two of us. Maurice, being senior was given first choice. He was certainly interested but after a week finally decided against the move largely because his daughter was upset at the prospect of leaving England. So the choice was left to me. Well! it's not an easy thing to decide to tear up all your roots for ever. I was given a week, until the day after August Bank Holiday to make up my mind. At the time my old school friend Benj. Farrar, and his wife and son Paul were staying with us. We had been out with them all day on the Bank Holiday (i.e. Val, me and John. Peter was away on the Merchant Taylor's Scout Camp) and by evening of that day Val and I had not made up our minds what to do. The Farrars knew all about our problem so after they had gone to bed we settled down to decide one way or the other. The factors to be taken into consideration were

(1) Although the Australian salary appeared to be better than what I was receiving, it had to be adjusted for the fact that the Australian pension was less than half the English pension and was moreover contributory. No contributions for pensions were payable in England. Even more important was the fact that £1 English was worth £1.25 Australian. I reckoned in 1938 that the Australian offer was in effect worth £300 to £400 (Australian) more than I was receiving in England. I have just confirmed the estimate by a recalculation. So it could never be thought that the salary I was offered could play a major determining part in the decision.

(2) The probability of greater responsibility was attractive.

(3) A major appeal was the opportunity of being in at the start of a new scheme and its subsequent development.

(4) The opportunities for Peter and John would be better in Australia.

(5) I was satisfied that we were on the verge of war and disgusted at the lack of evidence that people were willing to do anything about it. My own quite minor contribution was to become an air-raid warden. No-one else in the office did even that much. It seemed sensible to get out of the country while we could.

After another long discussion, in which we went over all the matters we had already discussed several times, we finally decided that I should accept the offer.

The next day I reported to Epps that I was willing to go for £A1,750 p.a. I saw the official Secretary at Australia House and provided him with the necessary facts to send to Australia.

We then went off for a holiday to a place about 15 miles from Cherbourg in France. We sailed third class on the Aquitania. The fares were £1 – third class, 30 s. – second class and £2 – first class including lunch, tea and dinner. We were given a four-berth cabin. This adventure was a great success and both the boys enjoyed every minute of the trip. I remember Val saying as the English coast receded from view, 'I'm glad we are not just leaving for Australia'.

We eventually got to a hotel and were duly installed. The food in the hotel was rather meagre. I could not understand why some of the French people had much better and more varied food than we did. I discovered later that they paid extra for things they ordered beforehand.

Anyway the holiday was thoroughly enjoyed by all. We spent some time on the beach and travelled around the area by bus. We also explored Cherbourg. We encouraged Peter to do the bit of shopping that was necessary in order to practice his French.

We had booked to stay for three weeks but after a week I got a cable to say that I had been appointed to the Australian job as 'Commonwealth Actuary', so we returned the next day after booking a passage to Southampton on the 'Empress of Britain' – this time in the second class.

I reported to Australia House where all necessary arrangements for our departure were made including berths on 'R.M.S. Orama' due to leave

Tilbury on 22nd October 1938. We had in fact six weeks to get ready for the departure.

Epps agreed that I could absent myself from the office as much as necessary in order to do all that had to be done, including the sale of our house. Through a local agent we found a buyer.

It was at this time that Hitler got really nasty over Czechoslovakia and Chamberlain had to fly to Germany to have talks with him.

In spite of having resigned as an Air Raid Warden because of my impending departure, I was asked to help when the Government decided to issue gas masks. I worked hard for a week on this job at some school in Harrow. I was surprised to find what awkward heads a few people had. The masks as supplied just would not fit to give complete protection. I found out that by adjusting the straps I could usually provide some sort of a fit. In fact I became the expert and I spent my time attending to all the difficult cases.

One of the good signs was the number of people who said how they admired those of us who had trained to become Wardens. It was some satisfaction to know that I had done the right thing and that there were signs of possibly better public response and co-operation in future.

Of course the effect of all this scare around the Munich Crisis was that the people who had contracted to buy our house reneged. The agent wanted me to sue them but I refused to throw money away. Anyway on the last morning before our departure I went into the office to say good-bye to everybody. I met a neighbour on Kenton Station and he asked if we had sold the house. When I said 'no' he enquired how much I wanted. I dropped £100 on our previous asking price and he said at once 'I'll buy it'. And he did. I gave Uncle Joseph a Power of Attorney before leaving. Later on the Estate Agent claimed a commission on the sale of the house for which he had found a defaulting buyer. My uncle wrote and told me the trouble he was having. So I cabled back 'do what you like'. I think he paid the commission.

For two nights before our departure we stayed with Uncle Joseph in Gayton Road nearby. On the morning of our departure we got a taxi to take us all including Uncle and Auntie to Fenchurch Street Station for our departure by special train to Tilbury. Maurice Knowles and his wife were there. Ruth (my sister) and Harold, Lucy and Elizabeth Emmerson were also there, with a view to travelling down to Tilbury with us. I have a feeling there were other people at the station but I have now, 38 years later, forgotten who they were. We arrived at Tilbury Docks in no time and found 'R.M.S. Orama' standing there waiting for us. The whole party went aboard, inspected our cabins and much of the ship. Eventually the departure time arrived and all visitors were ordered ashore. Then came the sad part. We were all looking over the side towards Ruth, Harold, Lucy and Elizabeth, Auntie and Uncle, who were standing in a group on the wharf. Gradually the ship moved away and as it did so I remember Ruth moving behind the others with her back to us where she obviously started to weep.

By this time of course Peter and John had become acquainted with almost every part of the ship and wanted to take us around. But we wanted to be quiet for a while. We watched the party on the wharf for some time but when the details of their faces became indistinct we moved away. We just wanted to sit quietly by ourselves for a while.

The Voyage – 1938

I think the first thing we did was to have a wash and then go down to lunch. We were allocated a table at which Val, I and Peter sat. Much to his disappointment John had to take his meals in the children's dining room, but he quickly settled into those quarters. At the time of our departure Peter was fourteen and John seven. After lunch we went to our cabins to unpack. The boys were in a cabin that backed on to ours. The cabins were of the old-fashioned Bibby type.

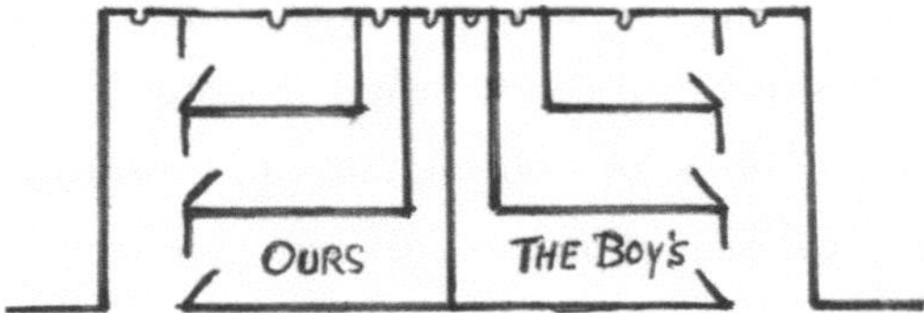

The U's represent port holes. So each cabin had a port hole. There was no air conditioning as on modern liners. As a result the cabins got pretty hot in the tropics. The long narrow passage to the port holes in our cabins were used mainly for airing washing. None of the cabins on our deck had private bath rooms which we have always had since when travelling by sea.

We entered into all the activities on the ship including deck quoits, deck tennis, swimming etc. Both John and Peter enjoyed the bathing. In fact John finally learnt to swim on the voyage.

Our first port of call was Gibraltar. Here we went ashore and hired a curious sort of trap to drive us round the town.

Our next call was Toulon. Val had not been too well for some days so she stayed aboard while I took the boys ashore. We had booked on a trip by coach to Le Lavendue where we wandered around, had lunch and, I seem to remember, John bought some miniature toys. In 1944 this was one of the places where the allies landed for the invasion of Southern France. At one point on our journey in the coach an Australian girl with us spotted a clump of gum-trees and insisted that the coach should stop. When she got off she danced barefooted around the trees. It was then that I realized for the first time what an affection Australians have for their eucalypts.

After our return to Toulon we sailed on to Naples passing between Corsica and Sardinia on the way. At Naples there were two trips on offer. (1) To the top of Vesuvius, or (2) to visit the excavated site of Pompeii at the foot of Vesuvius. Peter was given the choice and we were glad when he named the second alternative.

We all found it very interesting. I was particularly impressed by the ruts, made by the wheels of Roman chariots in the paved streets. At one locked museum Val and John were not allowed to enter but they let Peter go in with me. On view were a number of pornographic artefacts and paintings.

Afterwards the ship sailed down the west coast of Italy and at night we had a splendid view of the Stromboli volcano – all fiery red. Later we landed at Port Said where we went ashore to inspect a store named Simon Artz. I even bought a watch. We were all intrigued by the Egyptians selling various articles and especially by the Gulli Gulli man who produced live chickens from all sorts of places.

We next journeyed to Aden and then to Colombo where we stayed for a day. It was too far to take John by car to Kandy with me and Peter so Val stayed with him around Colombo, visiting Mount Lavinea.

Peter and I found the trip to Kandy very interesting because neither of us had visited an Asian country before. I remember we saw men working in paddy fields who, when we stopped to take a photo, came running out to be tipped. At Kandy we were taken to a good hotel for lunch. A servant helped us to descend from the bus, another showed us the way into the hotel, another took our hats, a fourth took us to the lavatory and finally polished the seat.

They all, not to mention the ones who served our lunch and there were several of those, and others who helped us out of the hotel and those who eventually showed us around the Temple of the Tooth, all expected tips.

I remember one strange sight and two incidents on the way back. The strange sight was the open fronted barn-like places that served as shops in the villages. The first incident occurred when we were driving through a village. A dog ran into the road and much to my disgust the driver of our car deliberately tried to run over it. Later the driver annoyed me again when I enquired about the things which boys held out on trays and tried to sell to us at every village where we stopped. I think they were betel nuts, sprinkled with lime and something else. He took some of the stuff from one boy and gave it to me to taste saying to the boy 'I'll pay you when I come back'.

~

We now set out for Fremantle. Early in the voyage I had been appointed by the passengers as the Treasurer of the Entertainments Committee. I think I was shanghaied into the job by either Herbert Brookes (who had been a member of the Tariff Board, the A.B.C. and other public activities) or Tom Dunbabbin (ex-editor of the *Sydney Telegraph* and returning from the position of Australian News Agency representative in London). I had, very early, become friendly with these two passengers. My job was to collect all the money that was subscribed by competitors in the various games and also the money raised in the sweepstake on the Melbourne Cup. Altogether I collected about £700 on the voyage, which I was glad to pass into the safe hands of the purser at the earliest opportunity. Out of the takings a certain proportion had to be given to some charity for seamen. No-one objected to this. I have forgotten what the percentage was but I remember I thought it was too much. Was it a third or a quarter? I do not know.

I now wish to tell the story of the Melbourne Cup. Never having been a racing man I do not think I had ever heard of the Melbourne Cup. Moreover I had never before been an organiser of a sweepstake nor indeed had I even bought a ticket in one. This was partly a relic of my Non-conformist

Conscience of which traces still remain today. Moreover I had learnt from my training in mathematical probability how to calculate the true value of a ticket in a sweepstake. Finally I had better uses for my money.

Anyway I collected some £300 or £400 for this event alone and the Committee had decided what the first, second and third prizes should be after allowing for the rake off. The Purser was always careful to see that he got every penny of it. Everyone knew when the race was to be run because I learnt it was always on a certain Tuesday in November. Well the day for the race eventually arrived.

By noon (Melbourne time) on that day we did not even know the names of the runners. The Wireless Operator had been trying for hours to get the list but for some reason he could not make contact. He still did not know the names of the runners at the time when the results of the race came over the wireless. Fortunately the passengers were ignorant of our dilemma. What should the Committee do? I wanted to refund the subscriptions but the Purser had his eye on all that money on which a deduction was due for the benefit of his Fund.

I eventually suggested and the Committee agreed to publish the results of the sweepstake as follows:

Position	Name of Horse	Name of Passengers	No. of Ticket
1	(a)	Mr	x
2	(b)	Mrs	y
3	(c)	Miss	z

Ticket numbers in the final column were found by putting the counterparts of all the issued tickets in a hat and drawing them out in the order x, y, z which enabled us to determine Mr, Mrs and Miss. The entry of the names of the horses was intended to provide an air of verisimilitude.

Mathematically it was perfectly fair, above board and the results were derived absolutely at random. Well perhaps not 'above board' because the passengers were never told about the subterfuge. But they all, and especially the winners, got all the fun they wanted; in fact just as much as they would have done if we had been able to tell them beforehand, the tickets which had drawn the various horses.

Australia – 1939

We had our first view of Australia at Fremantle about 26 November 1938. We were met at the docks by Sam Bennett (the Government Actuary of Western Australia) and a man named Hogue who represented the Deputy National Insurance Commissioner in Perth. We had heard from the wireless on the ship that the National Insurance scheme was meeting a lot of resistance from the public, and criticism in the newspapers. As we drove into the street the first thing I saw outside a newsagent's shop was a poster reading 'National Insurance abandoned'. That was not a very pleasant announcement seeing that I had come 12,000 miles to participate in the scheme. We were taken to some hotel in Perth for lunch. Bennett then departed and Hogue after showing us round the centre of the city took us by car to inspect the building of the Canning Dam of which the city was going to be very proud. I saw the finished dam in 1959 – 21 years later.

Our next port of call was Adelaide where we were not at all comfortable because the temperature was 113°F. In the ride in the train from Port Adelaide we passed through a lot of small houses. I was amazed because I had never seen so many corrugated iron roofs in my life. After a short stroll around the city we decided it would be more comfortable on the ship. As we entered the railway station to return to Port Adelaide, a man came and asked me if I was Mr Balmford. It was the Accountant (Flewellen) at the Adelaide Sub-Treasury. How he recognised me I do not know. All he might have known about me was that I would be with a wife and two boys. Perhaps it was my new Palm Beach suit that made me look like a travelling Englishman. He had missed me on the ship and was waiting there in the hopes of giving me a letter from the Treasury in Canberra. Flewellen and his wife then drove us back in his car to the ship.

We arrived in Melbourne the next day and three visitors came on board to greet us. They were Oswald Gawler, the State Actuary, with whom I became very friendly and saw a lot of in later years, Jackson the Actuary of the Temperance and General Assurance Society and Martin Bradley the Accountant at the Melbourne Sub-Treasury with whom I also eventually became very friendly during the War when I took on a number of economic controls and he was on my staff. Bradley had fixed us up with a room we could use at the Occidental Hotel until our departure at 5.30 by train for Canberra. After wandering around the city for a couple of hours we made our way by car to the station to catch the Spirit of Progress. It was a very modern new train of which the State of Victoria was very proud. We had to change trains at Albury and enter sleepers on the New South Wales railway. On arrival at Canberra there was a car waiting to take us to the Hotel Canberra where we were to live for six weeks. On entering the hotel the first person I saw was my old friend McKay who had for some reason missed us at the station. He had retired from the Insurance Department in London and was in Australia to assist in the introduction of the Insurance scheme. I knew him well. He took me round to the Treasury building and introduced me to officials in the Treasury and the National Insurance Commission.

I had to get down to work straight away. After two days I was asked to go to Sydney to give evidence before a Royal Commission on Medical Benefits. This Royal Commission was ill-fated from the start. A Judge who was the Chairman was ill for some time and then died. So far as I can recall the Commission never issued a report presumably because the Government suspended National Insurance. I don't think I was much help to them although I did clear up certain misunderstandings about the British scheme which existed in the minds of the Commissioners and several witnesses.

It was on this first visit to Sydney in December 1938 that I got in touch with Hedley who was in No.6 Squadron with me and, as I recounted earlier, with whom I spent Armistice Day in 1918. I had been advised to stay at the old Hotel Wentworth; which I did. As soon as I got into my bedroom I got hold of the telephone directory and looked up 'Hedley E.B.' (Ernest Barnes – in France we called him Barnees), and there was his name. So I immediately put through a call and when he answered I said in quite a casual tone 'Balmford here'. He replied 'I don't think I know you'. So I said 'Yes you do, isn't your name Ernest Barnes' and he agreed it was. I next said 'you will have to take your mind back a very long time'. But that was no use. I then said 'Think of No.6 Squadron'. And then I heard a tremendous roar. I met him the next afternoon and went around to his place at Killara for dinner. He was an electrical engineer in charge of constructional work on the NSW Railways. I saw a lot of him in the following years. Our two families became very friendly. I can still hear his voice when, after I had made some dogmatic statement, he would express his complete agreement by saying 'Absolutely, Walter, Absolutely'. He retired from the Railways in 1947 to take on the job of designing a new Sydney tram, and by Jove it was high time somebody did just that. Unfortunately he died in 1948 when carrying out tests on a knocked up prototype.

My immediate task, as Commonwealth Actuary, was to review the financial framework of the National Insurance Act which provided not only for sickness and medical benefits but also pensions for men at age 65 and women at age 60. The original actuarial estimates had been prepared by Fred Innes the Actuary of the Australian Mutual Provident Society (now known as 'AMP') and Sam Bennett the Government Actuary in Western Australia. With the help of an actuary (Wheatley) from the Australian Mutual Provident Society, two men from the Treasury and another from the Department of Customs (Hicks) who had sat several times for Part I of the Institute of Actuaries examinations, I got down to the job. I hired a calculating machine from a firm in Sydney. The end result of these independent calculations was to confirm with one or two minor reservations what Innes had done (Bennett I discovered did not help him much).

I had meetings two or three times a week with the Insurance Commissioners – Jim Brigden, Dan McVey and Harold Green.

Brigden was an economist who at the end of active service in the 1914 War in Europe had gone to Oxford. He had been a Professor of Economics and prior to becoming Chairman of the Commission had been Director of an Industrial Development Department in Brisbane.

He was a charming and very able man. Even though I have now to be critical of him, I always liked him and we got on very well together. He was more suitable for running a 'think tank' than administering a difficult operation. In fact I don't think he had ever had hard experience in Government administration. He was the only member of the Commission who realized what the problems were that they faced – and there were many. The trouble was he became obsessed with them. We were having extreme difficulties with the doctors who showed no signs of being co-operative when the scheme came into force. There was wide public opposition to the scheme. The Country Party, while part of the coalition Government, was far from enthusiastic about the scheme unless farmers and graziers were excused from paying employers' contributions, even though they had nebulous ideas that the farmers themselves should get free benefits. The Trade Unions were opposed to the payment of contributions even by the employers and thought all benefits should be paid out of Consolidated Revenue.

Brigden's other problems were associated with the insurance of agricultural workers, seasonal workers (like shearers) and casual workers (like wharf-labourers). He never solved them because he would not listen to advice. He got nowhere and apart from wasting a lot of time he neglected other matters that should have had his attention.

After the War started Brigden went to Melbourne to establish the Munitions Department. He was not a success there and was only saved by his Deputy Jensen, who had been on this work during and ever since the 1914 War. Eventually he was appointed Economic Adviser to the Australian Ambassador in Washington. Here he was in a more suitable element and, I believe did a good job. But I shall never forget a remark he made to me when he called to say goodbye before his departure. He said 'Of course, I shall, in effect, be the Ambassador there'.

McVey, the Second Commissioner was originally a Post Office Engineer and had for a short time been a member of the Public Service Board. He was a good organiser. His main contribution was to gather together a very efficient staff but they sat around with little to do until the War broke out.

Green, the Third Commissioner was the only member of the Commission who previously knew anything about Social Insurance. He had served as Secretary of an early Parliamentary Committee on the subject. His interest in National Insurance had continued afterwards and he was heavily involved in much of the work leading up to the Insurance Act. Actually, until then, his job was Assistant Commonwealth Statistician. He tried hard to persuade Brigden to 'get a move on' but he had no success.

A little earlier I outlined some of the problems which faced the Commissioners and especially Brigden who could not get them off his mind and get on with the main job. In our discussions I argued that too much time was being spent on the unresolved problems. I suggested (and I think I was right) that the thing to do was to use our powers under the Act to issue an Order exempting all the difficult occupations which did not fit into the requirements of the Act. Our main objective should be to get the scheme working and then deal with these awkward occupations afterwards. The number of people involved was relatively small. As regards the general opposition from the public I maintained that at the start the public was contribution minded. At the end of the first six months during which contributions had been paid, the payment of benefits would start. The public would then become more benefit minded. This had been the experience in England in 1912.

Everybody was pointing out what they regarded as faults in the scheme. In fact we all knew that it was not perfect but entirely novel schemes like this one never are. As Brigden once said 'The best is the enemy of the good'.

Well! although there were a lot of discussions and proposals for amending the Act we got nowhere and shortly after the War broke out the three Commissioners left for Melbourne to take on war-time jobs and the members of the staff were dispersed among those Departments which would have to expand. Although the Insurance Act was repealed some years later there was no need for immediate repeal. It had never been proclaimed.

I have often been asked why the National Insurance Scheme was a failure. I have already indicated some of the reasons and I now summarize them.

(1) Brigden's concentration on difficulties, his lack of experience in administration and his eventual loss of confidence in the possible success of the scheme.

(2) The scheme, as designed by Sir Walter Kinnear, did not take into account the different conditions in Australia as regards agricultural, seasonal and casual workers.

(3) Brigden's refusal to accept any advice from his two fellow Commissioners and me.

(4) Negotiations with the doctors were not helped by some offensive letters which Brigden wrote to the Australian Medical Association. They were despatched before copies were shown to his colleagues. I told him just before he went to his war-time job that a letter he had written the day before to the A.M.A. had destroyed all hope of ever making a satisfactory arrangement with the doctors.

(5) The Treasurer (Mr R.G. Casey, later Lord Casey and Governor General) had by the end of 1938, lost faith in the scheme. He was always inclined to take more notice of the last person who had spoken to him. One Saturday afternoon he invited Brigden, and me, with our wives, to his house in Canberra for tea. After tea the three men adjourned to his study and there he told us that he was worried about the annual cost of the scheme (namely £2,000,000), especially as War appeared to be imminent. He also said that the Insurance Scheme was so unpopular that he had been advised that he would be likely to lose his seat (Corio) at the next election. He did not stand at the next election because he was sent to America as Ambassador but the seat was lost to Labor.

(6) The appointment of poor quality public relations people to organize support for the scheme. Brigden of course interfered with the arrangements and insisted on his own ideas of the type of propaganda to be used. I think some of their joint efforts made it still more unpopular.

For instance Mr Casey was made to say in a talk to wives on the radio 'And do you know that if your husband is sick he will receive the magnificent sum of fifteen shillings a week until he is better in order that the family can be kept in comfort'. I heard neither the speech nor a recorded version of it which Arthur Calwell (a war time Labor Minister) told me he had secured. I think I have reproduced the words he quoted to me fairly accurately. Mr Calwell made full use of the record when Mr Casey put up for election again in 1949, by which time fifteen shillings a week was beginning to look pretty paltry.

Among those who were appointed to publicize and explain the scheme was a person who was a consultant who advised employers on the formation of Superannuation Schemes. Some people thought it was not a suitable appointment because of the possible conflict between his private work and his public job. He travelled all over Australia explaining the scheme to employers and employees. He was thus in a position to assess the extent of the opposition to the scheme and I think that it was the reports which he brought back to Canberra that influenced Brigden to lose all confidence in the success of the scheme.

(7) Shortly before he became Prime Minister in 1939 Robert Menzies had resigned from the Lyons Cabinet in protest against the failure to push ahead with the scheme. At least that is what he said, but most people thought it was a political device to lead him to the Prime Ministership.

(8) The public did not think of the benefits they might receive. They thought only of the contributions they would have to pay.

(9) The payment of contributions by the employers was not popular with them nor even with the trade unions who rightly claimed that the costs would be passed on in increased prices and thus be a further burden on top of the workers' own compulsory contributions.

(10) In fact nearly everybody seemed to be against the Scheme including the Country Party whose attitudes I have outlined earlier.

~

The question now arose as to what I should do. For some time I had been having talks with the United Kingdom High Commissioner (Sir Geoffrey Whiskard) about the position in which I found myself owing to the probable abandonment of National Insurance. He was sympathetic and reported to London. But we both realized that owing to promotions which had taken place down the line in my old Department following my departure there were problems involved if I wished to return. I had never actually resigned from the Department. I was almost regarded as a seconded Officer because I had been granted what was called 'Approved Service'. This meant that when I retired from the Australian Public Service I would pick up the pension I had earned during my service in England.

About the time the War started, there was a nebulous sort of arrangement that if the outlook had not improved within six months I should return to England. When the War broke out Sir Geoffrey asked me to go round and see him for a further discussion. His advice was that it was better for me to stay in Australia. He thought the Australian Government would be in need of specialist help and would find me something useful to do. He suggested that if I returned to England at once I would certainly be offered a war-time job but it would not be as responsible nor as interesting as what would be available in Australia where there was a shortage of top executives. He finally suggested it might not be wise to take two young boys back to England in wartime.

In the end I accepted his advice because it was in line with what I had been thinking. The result was I stayed and tried to help in the war effort in Australia. When it was all over both Val and I had settled in so well that we have had no wish since to return to England for good. Both Peter and John have been of the same view.

I spent the first two weeks of the War in clearing up my papers. The Secretary of the Treasury gave me two or three jobs (including reviewing a memorandum on financial control by the British Treasury which he used to extend his own methods). We had discussions about what I was to do. Eventually he gave me the choice of various types of jobs of which three were:

(1) taking over the administration of Capital Issues Control, which was just about to be introduced;
(2) going to live in Melbourne and doing a liaison job between the Defence Department in Melbourne and the Treasury; and
(3) taking over the Superannuation Board, of which I was a member.

The last named had no appeal to me. As regards the second I was certainly loath to move to Melbourne having settled very comfortably into a house in Canberra. I found the first offer attractive. For one thing my experience in financial management and the investment of the Insurance Funds in England would be a help. I had done work on the issue and redemption of Government securities for the British Treasury and as a Department we had been invited to express our views on interest rates. Moreover I had made a thorough study of Company Law for the examinations of the Institute of Actuaries. Altogether I could not think of anything else that might be available which would enable me to use whatever skills I had managed to acquire. But most of all I fancied the job would be interesting. So I agreed to take it.

I think that what I have just completed probably includes the most interesting part of my life; at least it seems so to me. What follows deals with my experiences during the Second World War and afterwards until my retirement. I deal with this portion quite briefly.

Canberra – 1939–58

When we arrived in Canberra at the end of 1938 the population was around 10,000. It remained close to that figure until a few years after the end of the War, when development recommenced. Thereafter the population grew rapidly.

We fell in love with the place as soon as we arrived there, even though it was really a glorified country town. We had the open country at the end of the street where we lived. We had the facilities of a modern city – electricity, water and sewerage – which were certainly not available in most country towns in Australia. We missed many of the things we had enjoyed in London – its historical associations, the theatres, the extensive transport facilities, nearby holiday resorts and the proximity of the European continent. In fact the only things I objected to in Canberra from the outset were the absence of a Parliamentary vote, and the bureaucratic control of Canberra without a Local Government Council elected by popular vote. It is true that there was an elected Advisory Council but it had very little influence on whatever was done. I still believe that though the management of Canberra was autocratic it was certainly benevolent. The citizens of Canberra could never be expected to provide for all the attractions of a worthwhile Capital City of which everybody could be proud. All Australians would share in the eventual heritage and all Australians should pay for it. On the other hand, the citizens could not be allowed to have control of the money available for development and use it for whatever they fancied.

We had discovered on the voyage to Australia that most people regarded Canberra as a joke or worse still an excrescence. They told us exaggerated stories about life in Canberra, the unduly benevolent treatment of the residents, the waste that took place, the segregation of the inhabitants according to salary and the isolation of Canberra from the rest of Australia.

There was not much substance in any of these stories. It was true that the people were roughly segregated according to salary. But they went to the houses for which they could afford to pay the rent just as much as people were segregated between Richmond and Toorak according to their ability to pay the requisite rents or mortgage payments. It always struck me as curious that people should complain that Canberra was isolated from the rest of Australia. Every capital city in Australia is very much separated from the rest of the country and suffers accordingly. To be equally provocative one could say that Sydney does not think much of Melbourne, that Melbourne can be rude about Sydney, that Brisbane is little more than an outback town, that although Adelaide prides itself on its respectability what else has it got, that Perth is so remote that its citizens have no idea what is happening elsewhere and that Hobart is the forgotten city that only survives with the help of substantial Commonwealth subsidies. I am prepared to concede that I have exaggerated but the statements have got some relation to the facts as they were in 1938. Things are better today. Nevertheless the views of other capital cities about Canberra were never right. There was always more intellectual life, per head of population, in Canberra than anywhere else in Australia. And as a result of the increased facilities since the War, the coming of the National University, the greater development of the Commonwealth Scientific and Industrial Research Organisation and the arrival of many specialist Commonwealth Departments including the National Library and the National Art Gallery, the advantage is still more in favour of Canberra. It seems to me that the mind of Canberra (and I don't mean the political mind) leads the continent. If there is any remoteness today it is remoteness from Canberra. By the way, the reader should be reminded that I have already admitted to a certain amount of exaggeration.

Faults there certainly were in the administration of Canberra. As an example I will take the case of housing. If a person was fortunate enough to acquire a block of land he had to get his building plans approved. But when the so called 'Proper Authority' – who in fact was an individual – could be persuaded to give his approval was beyond anybody's ability to determine. He would sit on an application for months and months before then he could even be induced to look at it. I never knew the reason for this treatment. Perhaps his instructions were to delay building as much as possible. But everybody thought it was just the nature of this particular officer. If, in the end, he could not delay any longer he could always find something wrong with the proposed building and this would most likely be due to his ignorance about changing building styles. On the other hand, one has to admit that a tight control over new buildings led to orderly development and that the 'Proper Authority' is to be commended for ensuring that Canberra avoided the ugly and haphazard development in some parts of the other cities in Australia.

I remember standing one evening in about 1954, at what is called 'the City' in Canberra, talking to a man who had been the 'Proper Authority' from the start of Canberra until his retirement about three years previously. He looked up at an office block of about four stories that had just been completed and said to me, 'They would never have erected that monstrosity if I had still been on the job'. It was the first high building that had ever been erected in Canberra. That story, in effect, illustrates what might be regarded as the principal feature which originally distinguished Canberra from other cities. Trees had been planted everywhere and people who visited Canberra carried away the memory of a city of beautiful trees. On leaving most cities of the world (including Australia) people remember the tall buildings. But the tall buildings are by now all over the place in Canberra and no 'Proper Authority' could have stopped that happening.

~

The first occupation of Canberra by the Commonwealth Government took place in 1927. Development had been halted in 1931 as a result of the depression but by 1938 conditions were right for a fresh start. Then came the War and that put a stop to any more development for ten years. We lived there through those ten years and for another ten years until 1958. It was a fairly hard life during the war years but the rationing and shortages were no worse than anywhere else in Australia. We were thrown back on our own resources for entertainment and relaxation and by and large most of us managed quite well. Both Val and I played golf although our hearts were in our mouths every time a high lofted ball got off course into the uncut rough because we knew we would have difficulty in purchasing a replacement. In summer our petrol allowance enabled us to get to the Murrumbidgee River once a month for a picnic and a swim. There was always plenty of gardening to be done and we kept ourselves in vegetables and mostly in fruits. In winter we could keep warm by endless chopping of wood for burning inside the house.

I think John suffered the most from the effects of the War on life in Canberra. Good toys simply did not exist and even the poor quality ones were not in adequate supply. We did what we could to meet the needs of a young boy. Another thing was that the average wear and tear on clothes made it difficult for John because good new clothes could not be bought. It must have been after four years of war that he was badly in need of a new raincoat but they were simply not obtainable. Yet I remember that when one day we were exploring a store in what Peter had christened 'the last outpost of the British Empire – Bungendore' we came across a cape made of some sort of waterproof material which looked like dirty, stiff, crumpled cardboard. We bought it for him and it did some sort of service for a year or two. I remember that in this remote store we also bought a good supply of Schweppes Pure Lime Juice, the quality of which is not even produced today. All they make now is Lime Juice Cordial.

It was a healthy life in Canberra and an ideal place in which to bring up children. There would be a short patch of very hot weather in summer, but nothing like so hot or so humid as Sydney. In winter the days could be cold (but not so by English standards). However on most of the cold days the sun shone brilliantly whereas in a Melbourne winter you get more dull days than sunny ones.

One of my first problems after arriving in Canberra was to make arrangements for the education of Peter and John. Having been influenced at first by the argument about the remoteness of Canberra I am afraid I thought it was not a place in which a child should be educated. So after looking at King's School in Parramatta and North Shore School in Sydney, we sent Peter to Geelong Grammar. I think now we sent him to the right place for the wrong reason. Our only regret is that he never seemed to live at home, except during holidays, after we came to Australia. He stayed at school until he was 18 when he enlisted in the Air Force. He eventually went to Temora on a flying course. It was then, for the first time that I realized what my own parents had gone through when I joined the Royal Flying Corps. I know that Val and I felt considerable relief when he was knocked out of flying because of air-sickness. At the end of the War, Peter went to do Law at the University of Melbourne and eventually became a solicitor.

As regards John, I was talked into sending him to Canberra Grammar School. Although I believe the school has since improved out of all recognition it was not a good school in 1938. It was poorly equipped and the qualification of some masters was I think 'failed matric'. The position got worse during the War. Eventually in 1942 the School, as a result of a threatened take-over by the Air Force was planning to move to Cooma in New South Wales. I did not see why I should pay for John to be a boarder in a poor school at a remote place. So I went to have a talk with the Headmaster of the local Primary School. He was willing to take John but would not promise to get him into the High School in the next year, except on his merits. It was a great disappointment to John because he had grown up in the Grammar School with rather a poor opinion of the Primary School. We did our best to help him to bear this burden and he eventually settled in quite well. His record was good, he got into the High School without difficulty and was happy there. We had given up all thought of sending him to Geelong Grammar because war-time taxation had become very high and school fees had increased. Moreover the government was threatening, because of transport difficulties, to prohibit inter-State train travel to school. In later years John agreed that I had done the right thing in removing him from the Grammar School. The next problem arose when the time came for him to go to the university. He wanted to go to Sydney where most of his friends were going. I insisted that he should go to Melbourne because, as I explained to him, we were not going to start one son off in Melbourne and another in Sydney. I agreed they might diverge in the future but I did not wish to be the one who had caused a separation. John afterwards also agreed with this decision. He finally went to the University of Melbourne, did a Commerce course and set out to become a Chartered Accountant.

Official Activities in War Time – 1939–45

Throughout the Second World War I was almost entirely occupied with the administration of war-time financial controls – all so different from my experiences during the First World War. The first and most important of these Controls was Capital Issues. Others which followed were:

(1) Building;

(2) Cash Orders and Hire Purchase;

(3) Stock Exchanges;

(4) Land Sales; and

(5) Marine War Risks Insurance.

A detailed description of any of these controls would be out of place here, so I will only say that:

(1) in Capital Issues we controlled the registration and issue of capital by companies, the borrowing of money by individuals and companies, and rates of interest.

(2) in Land Sales Control we had difficulties in attempting to peg the price at which land and buildings could be sold. We were reasonably successful for two years but eventually the 'black market' defeated us.

The administration of these controls involved a lot of hard work and for the first four years of the War I was back in my office on most nights until ten or eleven o'clock and sitting alone in the building on Saturdays and Sundays. The solitary weekends provided the only chance I had to do any thinking about the problems which had arisen during the previous week.

Advisory Boards of prominent businessmen were appointed to help me with most of the controls. They were especially helpful during the first few months of each control when my own knowledge of the subject matter was rather limited. In Capital Issues Control, for instance, neither I nor the Advisory Board knew exactly how we were to tackle the problems nor on what principles we should work. When the Commonwealth Treasurer presided over the first meeting of the Board the only view which he expressed on policy was that we should not do anything to increase unemployment which, at the beginning of the War, was already too high to be acceptable. As a rough guide to the policy which gradually evolved I would say that for the first two years we approved Capital Issue proposals which we thought would not interfere with the war effort. But later, and especially after the Japanese entered the War, we were only interested in propositions which would directly assist the war effort.

When capital issues control first started I did not look forward to so many interviews with all the important people who came to see me. I used to wonder what questions I could ask to ascertain the true facts and how I could reach a sensible decision about the matters raised. Very soon I learnt or discovered the answers to most of their arguments for the approval of their propositions. Sometimes they had good reasons for approval and I suppose in those cases it was usually granted. But very often their arguments were fallacious and those are the ones I came to recognise. I, of course, realized that if I had been in their shoes and sitting on the other side of my desk, I would also have been wanting to do the very things they did. But on my side of the desk I had a clearer knowledge of what was necessary for the war effort. What most people did not realize was that the things that mattered were the three M's – money, manpower and materials. Of these, money was the least important. In fact we were only restricting its use in order to prevent it being used for acquiring materials and using manpower which could be much better employed in the war effort.

Another aspect which many applicants did not realize was that we had sources of information unknown to them. We consulted specialist Commonwealth and State Departments who were often able to give us information not available to the applicants. I had my correspondents in both UK and USA. We had to be careful not to disclose our sources of information because they would dry up if they suspected that we were blaming them for an unfavourable decision. I will mention two particular cases where we were better informed than the applicants. In both cases it was proposed to purchase large second-hand equipment in USA, one to make cement and the other textiles. We were confidentially advised from America that the plant was pretty well worn out and in any case was being replaced because it was outmoded. We were heavily pressed to approve and, owing to a mistake by import control, we eventually did. In both cases the plant had to be scrapped and replaced within two or three years.

We had difficult problems when two competitive companies in the same field proposed to manufacture a particular substance which was definitely in short supply and badly needed in the war effort. This sort of thing happened twice. To make it worse we knew that one company could make all that was required and that after the War the normal demand would not support two manufacturers. On both occasions this happened, I tried tactful discussions with one of the parties. Each time my problem was eased by the party indicating that it suspected that its competitor was about to do the same thing. This enabled me to suggest that this would be unfortunate because it might result in over-development. They even agreed but were not anxious to approach the other party. Saying that it was my job to stop this sort of thing happening in wartime, I wondered if I could put out feelers to the other people without giving much away about their own intentions. After this exchange of ideas I seemed to gain their confidence and I was authorized to act. This happened as I say on two occasions in exactly the same way and both of them finished up in the same way – the parties met and made an amicable arrangement.

I have recollections of many episodes during my administration of the Capital Issues Control but I will recount only a few of the more interesting ones.

I should first explain that although the National Security Act provided penalties for non-compliance with the Capital Issues Regulations, we rarely prosecuted anybody. In the first place, we were able to rely on the fact that:

(1) under State law a Company which made a capital issue or gave a charge over its assets was obliged, within one month, to lodge details with the Registrar of Companies; and

(2) a mortgagee of land was obliged, in order to protect his interest, to lodge his mortgage with the Registrar of Titles.

So far as I can recall these officials did not have the power to refuse to act if a transaction had not been approved by us but after discussions and correspondence they certainly did their best to see that approval had been obtained. We were satisfied that on the whole people complied with the Regulations. An apparent loophole in the administration was that it would have been an impossible task for us to follow up and check that applicants had complied with the statements made in their applications; in other words, although they declared that the capital raised would be used for a particular purpose, that they had not used it for something else. Our main sanction against action of this sort was that most applicants had to return to us again and again. When they did we could usually spot any departure from their earlier undertakings. As a matter of fact applicants rarely told us lies but they did not always tell us all the facts.

Here is my selection of a few of the more interesting examples:

(1) During the War and for some years afterwards it was the policy under Capital Issues Control to restrict all expansion by retail traders. The same policy was adopted by the Commonwealth Bank in its directives to the Trading Banks regarding overdrafts. Shortly after the end of the War a large retail trading company with many branches had embarked on a vast developmental programme. To do this the company had been granted a substantial overdraft by its banker. It then applied to us for consent to

an issue of capital to reduce its overdraft. This was ridiculous because we knew they ought not to have secured the overdraft. We discovered that one of the directors of the trading company was also a director of the bank which had granted the overdraft. The inference was obvious. Such a blatant defiance of the directives of the Commonwealth Bank could not be disregarded so the company's application was refused. But in this case the trading company was lucky while it was the Bank which suffered.

(2) In the early months of the War a Local Authority sought to borrow money to finance urgently needed kerbing and guttering. A few months later another similar application followed from the same authority. On enquiry they admitted that they had spent the money on a swimming pool. I don't know when they were eventually able to get the kerbing and guttering done.

(3) We were always a little suspicious of people who brought samples of their wares partly because the samples did not enable us to determine their case but also because they often wanted to leave their samples with us. One client, for instance, found that his samples of towels were too heavy to carry around any more. Anyway he did not leave them with us.

(4) Another client came into my room and did not say a word until he was seated on the other side of my desk, had opened his bag and taken out a number of small bottles. He then took the cork off one of the bottles and said 'Smell that, Petrol. We've found it'. I had seen many people who were going to find oil but who, on the advice of the Commonwealth Geologist, were fortunately never given the opportunity to do so. Even the few whose applications were approved never found anything. I did take the bottle and its contents did smell like petrol. So I said 'How do I know you did not fill this up at the nearest bowser'. I believe this chap was fundamentally honest. At least he did not say anything more until he had put his bottles back in his case. What he had found, I suspect, was another seepage of dirty oil and water of which we had had previous reports from the geologist.

(5) Another client brought photos of two sets of plants growing alongside. The plants in one set were robust and well developed. They had been

fertilized by some stuff he had produced. The other plants were small and drooping because they had not been treated. The stuff that had boosted the first lot had been extracted from tailings outside an old copper mine. Even to me the photos were an obvious fake, but he only pretended to be amused when I enquired whether there was any chance that he had applied the fertiliser to the wrong set. I suspected this man was a rogue and became convinced when he confessed that, without telling his prospective shareholders, he was actually going to make a fortune by extracting pure copper from the tailings. After he left and before he came back the next day for our answer, I got in touch with my next door neighbour Dr Dickson who was the Director of the Plant Pathology Department of C.S.I.R.O. He told me that there were only two pockets in Australia where there was any shortage of copper in the soil – one was in Albany in Western Australia, I don't remember where the other was. Anyway on this evidence we decided he had better go on using the stuff on his own vegetables.

(6) One of the cheekiest applications we received was from a well-known soap manufacturer. The general manager justified the need for further capital by saying (in 1947) that they had not increased the price of a tablet of soap since 1939. So I made the obvious enquiry as to whether the tablets were still the same size. Actually I knew they had been reduced because we used the stuff at home. He was a little embarrassed when he admitted to the reduction in size. It was in situations like this when you realized that you were in control. Matters became more difficult for him when I had a look at the Company's accounts which he had brought along. It was perfectly obvious, and he admitted it, that from the receipts from sales one third went in expenses, one third in dividends and the remaining third in advertising. I suggested that instead of raising more capital he should cut down his advertising. (I was interested to read, at the end of August 1976, that the Prices Justification Tribunal was dealing with a similar situation.)

(7) Since the beginning of Capital Issues control we had always refused to allow any hire-purchase company to raise more capital. But the general

manager of one such company asked me if we would object if they formed a number of new companies each with a capital of £2,500. I said we could not object because under the Regulations any company could raise an amount of £2,500 in any one year. But I suggested they would soon be in a mess if they tried to run their business through a lot of small companies. He was back in a year asking me to help them out of the tangle they had got into with all the companies they were trying to run.

(8) Several companies did express their gratitude to us for stopping their proposed expansion in 1951. The Treasury had advised us of a coming recession and as a result we were being very restrictive.

Another expression of gratitude came from the Clerk of a large Local Authority, which had received our consent to raise a loan. They had been promised the money by a lender before we gave consent. We had, for some time, been making periodic reductions in the rate of interest payable on new loans to Local Authorities. As the result of a further reduction in the rate before this particular loan was finalised the lender refused to proceed. The Clerk phoned me in great distress. I took his number and said I would ring back within an hour. I then rang the Commonwealth Bank in Sydney and told them the circumstances. They said they thought they could help by lending at the reduced rate if all the details I had been told were correct. I therefore rang the Clerk and told him to get in touch with a particular person at the Commonwealth Bank. I did not hear anything more about this matter until about five or six years later when I was attending a Rotary Club Luncheon in Sydney. A man at the same table recognised my name and introduced himself as the grateful Clerk. I should add that he was not the Clerk of the Council of the City of Sydney.

I do not propose to enter into any details about the other wartime controls except to mention that, as a result of allegations that I had been guilty of improper conduct in the administration of Land Sales Control, a Royal Commission was appointed to investigate the matter. It was all a storm in a teacup. The finding of the Royal Commission was that I had acted honourably and done nothing improper, whereas the person who had made the charges had certainly been guilty of misbehaviour.

Walter & Val, 16 July 1942, in Martin Place, Sydney, New South Wales.

For most of the war period the Commonwealth Treasurer was Mr J.B. Chifley. He was also Prime Minister from 1945–49. I first met him in 1939 when the Menzies' Government appointed him to the Capital Issues Advisory Board. He re-entered Parliament in 1941 and became Treasurer shortly afterwards. He was thus my boss from 1941 to 1949. But he was far more than that because of all the Ministers I served he was the only one whom I could regard as a friend. And I think he regarded me as a friend too because, although I make no claim that he turned to me for advice on matters other than those which were my concern, he used to give me his confidential thoughts, describe his problems and difficulties and seemed glad to have someone to whom he could just talk, and relieve his mind. He liked me to join him for a drink after six o'clock or to go for a short walk when he had eaten his lunchtime sandwiches. Everybody in the Treasury admired him for his intellectual ability, his vision, his capacity for hard work, his kindness and consideration for others. He had no pretentions. He was honest and reliable. I did not insist on written instructions from him because I knew I could rely on his word. He had a fabulous memory which he drew upon when considering any matter submitted for his instructions. By nature he was a simple man without ostentations of any sort. But I came to realize, after being with him on many occasions when he was interviewing people, that he had learnt the practical value of this attitude to life.

I have chosen two of my experiences with Mr Chifley which I think throw some light on his character.

The first incident occurred during a General Election when I knew that Mr Chifley was out on the dustings in the wilds of Queensland and could not be contacted. The Solicitor General phoned me to say that Counsel, who was to appear on my behalf in the High Court the next morning had advised that we could not win the case. What were my instructions? After some thought I told him we would withdraw from the case. I reported to Mr Chifley what I had done when he returned to Canberra. He immediately said 'I do not blame you because you had to make up your mind one way or the other but I would rather have fought the case and lost than give in'.

The other incident relates to a long closely reasoned letter which I submitted for his signature. As he seemed to be just glancing at the letter, I said, as he turned over to the third page and reached for his pen, 'That letter is politically red-hot, you ought to read it very carefully'. His reply was 'I have, ask me something about it'. And he had read every word. He was in fact a very fast reader.

Post War – 1945–58

Most of the controls finished shortly after the end of the War but Capital Issues Control continued until the end of 1953.

During 1944 and 1945 I had put in a lot of time drafting a Life Insurance Bill, which was presented to and passed by Parliament in 1945. I was appointed Insurance Commissioner, collected a lot of statistics and published an annual report on the working of the Life Insurance Companies. I was not very interested in this work and always regarded my position of Commonwealth Actuary as far more important. I had realized for some time that while most of the Life Insurance companies were perfectly sound, there were a few that, although rather weak, could with careful management be strengthened and brought to complete solvency. Besides these companies there were three which were already hopelessly insolvent and would have to be wound up as soon as possible. Over the next twenty years the doubtful group were carefully watched and they did attain a satisfactory condition. I caused investigations to be made into the three insolvent companies in order to collect the evidence to be put before the High Court in an application for their winding-up. In each case my application was granted. In fact I spent a lot of time after 1946 in the High Court dealing with these matters and challenges to the validity of the Capital Issues and other Regulations.

From 1947 to 1957 I was engaged in the actuarial work in connection with the Commonwealth and other Superannuation Funds. I had been a member of the Commonwealth Superannuation Board since 1939. I was also on the Board dealing with superannuation in Papua and New Guinea. This involved two visits to New Guinea.

In 1956 I was appointed a Commissioner on the Overseas Telecommunication Board. I really enjoyed the work on this Board mainly because it gave one a feeling of achievement instead of frustration which is the usual lot of a Public Servant. In 1959 the Commission made an extensive tour of Papua and New Guinea in order to inspect our various installations there with a view to a reorganization. Val came with me (at my expense) on this tour. We visited Port Moresby, Lae, Rabaul, Kavieng, Wewak, Madang and Garoka. I formed several opinions as a result of this tour. Australia had in the first place only taken over Administration of the Territory for defence purposes. It seemed obvious to me that under modern war conditions the place had not much defence value. Moreover Australia was committed to granting independence to the Territories. In the meantime she was pumping money and resources into the place. This drain would increase rapidly in future and be beyond the capacity of Australia. As I write, Papua and New Guinea have recently been granted independence. It will be interesting to see if my fears materialize. While there I was appalled at the work of missionaries. The work was mainly performed by three groups, Methodists, Catholics and Jehovah's Witnesses, all in active competition for converts. So far as I could discern it was all a source of confusion to the natives.

Another interesting experience in this post-war period was the visit Val and I paid to England in 1948: the first since our departure in 1938. The principal reason for the trip was the Centenary Celebrations of the Institute of Actuaries in London. These included an International Congress of Actuaries at which I attended all the sessions. Val and I attended many social functions including a dinner at the Guildhall and an afternoon tea party at Windsor Castle. Val travelled to England by sea two months before I left by plane. I was in England for two months and Val returned home to Canberra two months after I got back. We spent a lot of time with her sisters and with mine. My father was alive at the time and we took him to Edinburgh in a hired car.

Although I had always intended to retire from the Public Service when I reached age sixty, I decided to stay on a little longer when the time came.

My main reason was that I was in the middle of various jobs which I wanted to complete or to see well on the way to completion. I involved my probable successor in the decision making in new jobs as much as possible because it would be his responsibility when the chickens came home to roost. Another reason for delaying my retirement was the likelihood that I would be asked to take on several directorships. I was really anxious to retire because, although I had enjoyed my official career in both England and Australia, there had throughout been a certain amount of frustration. In particular, I was continually giving advice on various aspects of National Insurance but nothing ever happened. So I settled for retirement on 31 December 1957 and that is the date on which I actually retired from the Commonwealth Service. In the following March we left Canberra and went to live in Melbourne where both Peter and John had been at the University and were now working, Peter as a solicitor and John as a Chartered Accountant.

This was another vital change in our life which we were reluctant to make. For two or three years before my retirement Val had been advocating an eventual removal to Melbourne so as to be near our sons. I was opposed to her suggestions; mainly, I said, because we had burnt our boats once and I had no wish to do so again. Then, when I was offered several directorships in Melbourne which would more than double my pension, I was all for going there. But, of course, Val had changed her views and had no wish to leave all her friends behind in Canberra. The discussions between us were always amicable and were easily resolved because we had both to admit that our minds had wobbled. It was no victory for me because Val got what she really wanted and has never regretted the move.

Retirement – 1958

I retained my commissionship on the Overseas Telecommunication Commission until the middle of 1959. When the end of my three-year appointment was approaching I was asked if I would take over the Chairmanship of the Commission. I agreed, but three weeks later I received a letter from the Postmaster General saying my appointment was not to be renewed and thanking me for my services. It seemed a bit rough but I received unofficially something of an explanation. There had always been a Treasury nominee on the Commission and I was the latest one. In the middle of 1959 the Commission was entering into heavy commitments for the construction of a new cable and the Treasury wished to have a more direct representative than a retired official who no longer lived in Canberra.

Before retirement I had agreed to take on the Chairmanship of the Legal and General Assurance Society Ltd., an English company which was to start life insurance business in Australia on 1 January 1958. It was an interesting experience especially as, although an actuary, I had never previously been associated with a life insurance company. I had been asked to suggest the names of possible directors. I chose Sir Alexander Fitzgerald in Melbourne and Stan Bryson in Sydney. I had known the former for many years: in fact he had been with me on the Capital Issues Advisory Board. He was the senior partner in a firm of Chartered Accountants in which our son John worked and eventually became a partner. Stan Bryson was an old acquaintance being an associate Member of the Institute of Actuaries and on the staff of the Commonwealth Bank. The membership of the Board was extended in later years to include other earlier associates of mine.

Walter in his retirement.

Walter C. Balmford – portrait. The author, left, with the artist, the well-known painter, Graham Inson (1923–2000), inspecting his portrait, which was commissioned by Legal and General Assurance Society Ltd., of which he was the first Australian Board Chairman from 1958. The portrait was later given to the Balmford family.

Drawing of Florence 'Val' Balmford, by H.R. Ham.

Portrait of Walter Balmford, by Graham Inson.

Legal and General Assurance Society Ltd. erected a new building, on the south-east corner of Collins and Queen Streets, Melbourne. In the photograph, Walter is demonstrating a model outside the new building to Lord Casey, then Governor General of Australia, he having opened the building on 27 November 1967. The company's Australian business was later taken over by the Colonial Mutual Life Assurance Society Ltd., itself later taken over by the Commonwealth Bank of Australia in 2000.

I enjoyed my association with the Legal and General and I think the Board contributed something to the solution of its major problems. I resigned from the Board at the end of 1972.

I also received an invitation to join the Boards of the Capel Court Group of Companies in Melbourne. I started with them on 1 January 1958. Once again this was a very interesting appointment. There were at the outset eight investment companies within the group. We started another investment company shortly after my appointment. In subsequent years we controlled six Unit Trusts, three Underwriting Companies, a Short-Term Money Market Company and finally what was called Capel Court Corporation. Just before my retirement from the group in March 1973 the Corporation absorbed the money-market company and all the underwriting companies. The most fascinating work was with the short-term money market. We borrowed vast sums of money, mostly at call, from Banks and other companies which had unused liquid funds and gave them a temporary lien over Commonwealth bonds which we owned. Our profits came from the excess of the interest we earned on our Bonds over that we paid to our lenders. The amount of the margin was subject to quite sudden and large variations. Our most difficult times were when the rate of interest on bonds rose. This had the effect of reducing the market value of our bonds. On two occasions, while I was on the Board, the sudden drop in market values more than offset the profit we had made in the previous year. The only way we could protect our position was, when we anticipated a rise in interest rates, to switch into the Bonds with the shortest outstanding terms (i.e. those near maturity whose market values would not be influenced much by the rise in interest rates). Unless we were clever enough to anticipate the coming change in good time we would find that there were no short-term Bonds available.

I also joined the Boards of A.E.I. Ltd. and its subsidiary Australian Electrical Industries. I cannot say that I found this association very satisfactory. A.E.I. had Australian shareholders but it was a subsidiary of A.E.I. in England which had paid far too much to acquire the operating company Australian Electrical Industries. It was a constant battle to make any profit at all and towards the end the company was continuously in the red. A large part of the trouble was due to domination by the Head Office in London. For instance A.E.I. (Australia) was formed in 1955 just before television commenced in Australia in 1956. The company was instructed by London that it should make Ecko TV sets on the same pattern as those in London and without a transformer. This instruction was against the advice of the Australian Company which knew that all other makes in Australia were installing transformers in their sets. Well of course from the start the dealers rubbished the A.E.I. sets claiming that they were dangerous and so they were if a person was careless in opening up the set.

We got, from State Electricity Commissions in Australia, orders to supply large generators. These were beyond the capacity of our Australian factories so we had to get them made by A.E.I. in England. They let us down time after time in the completion of the work, mainly because they concentrated on other more profitable contracts. But of course the Australian company got the blame from the Australian customers. In the end, when the generators had been delivered, London took its full costs and profits out of the contract price. The result was that, instead of the Australian company receiving a fixed and fair commission for the large amount of work in securing and servicing the contract, it was handed the meagre amount that was left after London had taken all it wanted. London had other nasty habits. They started exporting washing machines and refrigerators to compete on the market with the ones we were selling. The final blow came when they took over a cable maker in Australia and started selling their products in competition with our cables. So one of the other directors (A.V. Smith) and I signed, in the interests of the Australian shareholders, a letter of protest to the Chairman in London and suggested that their two other operating companies in Australia should be taken over by us. Their reply was to say 'no, but we will take you over'. This is what happened and the only decent thing they ever did was, in buying out the Australian shareholders, to pay them the same price for their shares as they had been charged when the issue was first made. This was generous because the market value of the shares was much below their issue price. I think this about ends the accounts of my business activities after 'so-called' retirement. I was glad when I finally relinquished all my appointments in 1973 because having reached the age of 76 I knew I was not as good as I used to be (that is, if I ever was any good) and I was finding the daily visit to the city by car very tiring even though I usually did not stay more than four hours.

I have already mentioned that we made our first visit to England in 1948. We went again in 1960, 1966 and 1972. The first of these trips was the 'grand tour' after retirement. We visited Hong Kong, Japan, Holland, England, Belgium, Germany, Austria, Italy, USA (New York and Chicago) Canada (Banff and Vancouver). When we were in Chicago we met the children, grandchildren and great grandchildren of my Mother's brother Nathan Crowther whom I referred to on pages 8 and 26. We stayed with his daughter Grace who is the wife of Peter Ronvic. It was a wonderful experience to renew a friendship with Grace and her sister Mary with whom I had spent many holidays as a child over fifty years previously. They didn't even know or had forgotten that my second Christian name was 'Crowther'. John also stayed with Grace in 1967 and Peter, with his wife Rosemary and their son Christopher, followed suit in 1975. They also enjoyed the visits and carried away as many happy recollections of our American cousins as Val and I had done. We went to England in 1966 mainly to satisfy Val's sisters that – although she had been blinded in one eye, after suffering a detached retina in the previous year – she was otherwise in pretty good shape.

We spent most of the time in 1966 in England though we did go for a cruise along the Norwegian coast as far as the Russian border with my sister Olive and her husband Reg. On the return flight we spent several days in both Bangkok and Singapore.

The excuse for going again in 1972 was to celebrate our Golden Wedding. We arranged a dinner at the Hurlingham Club in London to which we invited many of the people mentioned in these memoirs. I give in Appendix A copy of some notes we sent to all our guests beforehand.

After this most enjoyable affair we flew with John to Vienna and toured by car around Austria, a bit of Germany and Switzerland. On the return flight from London to Australia we spent the first night in San Francisco and then flew to Fiji where we stayed for a week.

So now (August 1976) I am leading a very quiet life but still enjoying it. I go into Melbourne twice a week, on Mondays to meet for lunch at the Athenaeum Club with my old friend and colleague Norman Watt (ex-Secretary of the Commonwealth Treasury) and on Wednesday to attend the weekly meeting of the Melbourne Rotary Club.

Editors' Afterword

This family photo, taken in 1905 in Warrington, shows Walter (at the age of 9) in the rear with his sister, Ruth to the viewer's right. The front row shows his father, Edgar, at the age of 38 with Walter's younger sister, Olive and his mother, Mary, then aged 37.

Later, the family moved to the nearby village of Thelwall in Cheshire, close to the Manchester Ship Canal. Olive and her husband, Reg Leah later lived next door.

Before emigrating to Australia, Walter and his family regularly visited Thelwall, particularly at Christmas. In 1938, on the final visit before departure for Australia, all were involved in helping to dig an air raid shelter behind the house. Peter & John had been parked there while the packing-up took place.

After World War Two, Walter's mother having died, Walter and Val visited his father several times, as did his elder son, Peter, on one occasion, accompanied by his then wife, Glen.

John never saw his grandfather again.

On retirement from the UK Civil Service, Walter's colleagues presented him with a 9.5-mm ciné camera as a retirement gift. He decided to buy an identical camera for his father, with a view to exchanging films as part of keeping in touch. After the start of the war, films became unprocurable and only one film was ever exchanged.

The first communication, apart from the mail, was on 31 December 1950 on the occasion of his father's 80th birthday and of his sister, Ruth's 50th birthday. It was a disappointment. The call was made from Walter's office so that each family member would have a handset but this apparently caused problems and the number of extensions was reduced from four to two. It was expensive: there was a long delay for connection, the line was full of static and Val did not appreciate being told that Walter's family all had Australian accents.

Walter died aged 82 at home in Melbourne on 14 May 1979, survived by his wife, Florence (known as 'Val'). He had retained generally good health up to the time of his death.

His widow, Val died just over twelve months later on 30 May 1980, aged 85.

Walter and Val had two children, Peter, 1924 and John David, 1931.

John married Dagnija (Dani) Missins.

Peter, was twice-married, first to Glen Tomasetti, later to Rosemary Balmford AM. He died on 18 January 2005, aged 80, Rosemary on 8 August 2017.

Peter and Glen had two children. Their daughter, Clare, now Clare Bell, has a daughter Lina and is married to Eric Bell. Their son, Jonathan is unmarried.

Peter and Rosemary had a son, Christopher, who is married to Kym Ortenburg. They have two children, William and Grace.

Appendices

A. Balmford Family Tree

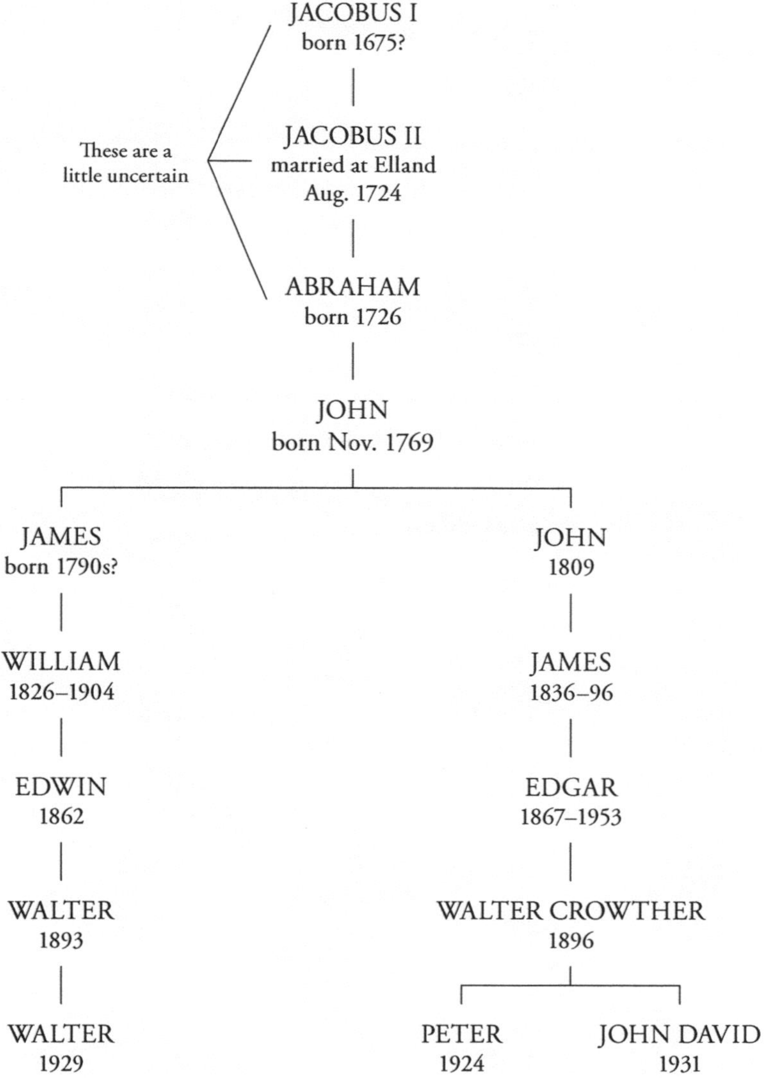

B. List of Authors

James Balmford		**Year of Publication**
(1)	*A short plaine dialogue concerning the unlawfulness of playing at cards*	1593
(2)	*Three Positions concerning the Lord's day*	1606
(3)	*A short catechism comprising the principal points of Christian Faith*	1607
(4)	*Carpenter's Chippes or simple tokens of unfeigned goodwill*	1607
(5)	*A short dialogue concerning the Plagues Infections* (I think this attempted to prove that the Plagues were due to man's Godlessness)	1603
Samuel Balmford	*Habakkuks Prayer*	1659
William Balmford	*The Seaman's Spiritual Companion*	1678

C. To Our Guests at the Hurlingham Club, London, 24 May 1972

As you come from so many different places in England and Australia and are not all known to one another, we thought it would be helpful to introduce you beforehand.

We hope the ladies will not mind the biographies being confined to the males because it is with them that our main associations arise.

(Miss) Cis Valantine[*] (Mrs) Hilda Sellwood) (Miss) Edith Valantine	These are Val's sisters who live in Sellwood South London. Edith was one of Val's bridesmaids and Hilda stayed with us in Melbourne in 1962–63. I am sure they will not mind my telling you that they are affectionately known to us as 'Les Girls'.
Walter Balmford Val Balmford	Our family known most to you.
Peter and Rosemary Balmford	Both are solicitors practising in Melbourne.
John Balmford	Bachelor of Commerce and Practising as a Chartered Accountant in Melbourne.
(Miss) Ruth Balmford	Walter's sister who was also one of Val's bridesmaids. She is now living in retirement near Oxford.

* Cis unfortunately died just before the dinner.

Olive and Reg Leah	Olive is Walter's sister. She and Reg live at Thelwall, near Warrington. They stayed with us in Melbourne in 1967–70. Reg, who has now retired, spent his working life in the wire industry. (Rylands- to those who know Warrington.) Curiously, Rylands established an offshoot of the same name in Newcastle in New South Wales. It was taken over by Broken Hill Proprietary (Australia's largest company) many years ago.
Eddie and Mary Balmford	Eddie is Walter's cousin. After doing mathematics at Oxford he became a Chartered Accountant and is still practising in Huddersfield Yorkshire.
Sir Harold and lady (Lucy) Emmerson	Harold and Walter were at school together. Even though he won all the scholarships around the place, Harold decided to enter the Civil Service at the same time Walter did (1914). Thereafter they were in digs together until Harold had to hold Walter's hand when Val and he were married (1922). Harold became the Director General of Manpower during the War and eventually Permanent Head of the Ministry of Labour. He is now retired and living in Berkhamsted near London.
Ben and Ethel Farrar	Ben and Walter were at school together. Walter's earliest recollection of him is meeting after school on three afternoons a week to go to the local baths together. They were very different from open-air baths and beaches in Australia. He was a headmaster of several schools but is now living in retirement at Swindon (Wilts.)

Maurice Knowles

Maurice is an Actuary and an old colleague of Walter's in the Government Actuary's Department. In 1950 he attended an International Conference in New Zealand (with Dennys – an earlier colleague of Harold Emmerson). They came to Australia afterwards and stayed with us in Canberra. We had an official conference with them on reciprocity for social service benefits. When Maurice attained 60 he decided to kick over the traces (which many of us would often have liked to have done). He retired on his 60th birthday and the next day flew to Austria to rub up his German at Innsbruck University. Thereafter he became a Courier taking parties walking, climbing and touring around the Austrian and Italian Tyrol. Val and Walter joined his party in 1960 and were knocked out by a climb on the first day. He is now permanently retired and living at Purley near London.

Ron and Joy Peet

Ron comes from Doncaster – UK not Victoria. After a period in the Army he gained his M.A. at Oxford in Theology. He then went to a Theological College in USA but decided not to pursue his intended vocation. So he returned to England and started with the Legal and General Assurance Society. He qualified as an Actuary after being transferred to Australia in 1956. In 1965 he became General Manager of the Society in Australia. He was pulled back to England three years ago and is now General Manager of the whole Society.

He lives at the Putney near London and being a member of the Hurlingham Club has arranged for the dinner.

Norman and Barbara Apthorp	Norman and Peter were at school together from 1930 to 1938 and remained close friends at their preparatory school and Merchant Taylors. Norman subsequently did physics at Cambridge and while attached as a Boffin to the R.A.F., hitchhiked by air from Rangoon to Canberra where he stayed with us for a fortnight (1946). On his return to England he performed Ron Peet's act in reverse. He became a clergyman of the Church of England and eventually moved to Australia. He is now Dean and about to leave Northam in Western Australia to become the Vicar of Kalgoorlie. He is at present on sabbatical leave. The Actuaries and other mathematicians will be interested to know that Barbara graduated in mathematics at Cambridge.
John and Elfie Knowles	John is Maurice's son. Elfie is Austrian. We first met John in 1936 when our two families had a holiday together at Woolacoombe, Devon. In 1946 the Carrier on which he was serving arrived in Sydney, so he joined us in Canberra at the same time as Norman was there. These two boys with John and Peter had memorable peach battles from the plentiful supply of ripe peaches in our garden. John returned to Oxford to do (we think) Modern Greats. He is now an expert in Organisation and Methods and lives at Purley.

David and Marjorie Wallace	David is a Cambridge Mathematician who afterwards joined the Legal and General. He became an Actuary and was sent to Australia about ten years ago. He eventually became General Manager when Ron Peet returned to England. He lives in Sydney, NSW.
Sid and Molly Caffin*	Sid joined Walter's staff in Canberra in 1946 and eventually qualified as an Actuary. He had pursued his earlier actuarial studies while serving as a Sergeant Major in New Guinea. The rank gave him more opportunity for study than he would have had as a commissioned officer. He succeeded as Commonwealth Actuary when Walter retired in 1958.
John and Anne Emmerson	John is Harold's son. He followed Peter and Norman at Merchant Taylors afterwards doing law at Oxford. He is now a partner in a firm of solicitors in the West End of London.
Leila St John	Leila is the widow of Reg. St John who was the General Manager in Australia of Legal and General before Ron Peet.

* Molly and Sid's departure was delayed and so they were not present at the Party.

D. Editors' Appendices

1. Updated Balmford Family Tree

This Appendix sets out an abbreviated family tree as it was perceived at the time of writing.

Walter's son, John had in about 1950 asked his then 83-year-old grandfather, Edgar (1867–1963), for whatever Balmford family details he was able to recall. These were duly provided in 1951, needless to say in hand-written form, showing some 50 or more Balmford individuals. Based on that document, as extended by Walter and John, the family tree, now on computer and with much other research, including by John's second cousin, David, has expanded to over 250 family names.

In October 1964, Walter had received a letter from another Walter Balmford (Walter 2, b. 1929), written on the company letterhead of Walter Balmford Ltd., Electrical Engineers of Birmingham, England. Walter 2 had read in an electrical journal of Walter's retirement from the Board of A.E.I. Ltd. (page 145) and had been intrigued to read a reference to a namesake. Neither family had any previous knowledge of the other but that letter started a correspondence which has continued, particularly on family tree matters, for a number of years. It was established that Walter 3 was a third cousin of Walter, each being a descendant of John Balmford (b. 1772), their mutual Great Great Grandfather. Walter 2 had himself had done much research into the family tree but had been very surprised by the appearance of a previously unknown (to him) branch of the family. Curiously, there was a marked similarity in first names of the contemporary family members. Walter 2's father was also Walter (Walter 3) (1893–1994, lived to 101 years!). His wife was named Florence. They had four sons – named Walter, John (dec'd), David and Peter. Walter's wife was also named Florence. They had only two sons, Peter (dec'd) and John David.

The family tree in this Appendix shows three further antecedents, described as 'a little uncertain'. More recent research using the internet appears to identify earlier Balmfords, with various surname spellings used at the time – Bamford, Bamforth etc. The current common forms are probably Bamford, Balmforth and Balmford. Spelling was less consistent in the earlier days. The pronunciation of 'Balmford' and 'Bamford' being seemingly identical.

2. *A Family Outing at Bolton Abbey, Yorkshire (c.1906)*

Photograph taken by Herbert Buckley – Walter's first cousin once removed.

Back row:
John Alfred Balmford – Walter's uncle (1870–1954)
His wife, Edith Balmford (1870–1955)
Edgar Balmford – Walter's father (1867–1953)
His wife, Mary – Walter's mother (1868–1947)
Alice Balmford – wife of James E. Balmford (1865–1944)
James Edward Balmford – Walter's uncle (1871–1950)

Middle row:
Ruth Balmford – Walter's sister (1897–1975)
Arnold Balmford – son of John A.Balmford (1895–1917)*
Walter Crowther Balmford (1896–1979)
Son of Herbert Buckley – Walter's second cousin
Daughter of Herbert Buckley – Walter's second cousin

Front row:
Son of Herbert Buckley – Walter's second cousin
Olive Balmford – Walter's sister (1903–1981)
Edith Balmford – daughter of John A. Balmford (1901–1931)
Edward Vernon Balmford – son of J. A. Balmford (1903–1988)
Pattie Mann – niece of Alice Balmford

* The two cousins served in the armed forces in France in World War I. They were in the same area of the country, although not necessarily at the same time. Sadly, Arnie did not survive. Walter did!

3. Arnie's Story

Walter's uncle Arnie (back row, fifth from right) in costume with officers.

The text of this contemporary newspaper clipping tells the story of Walter's uncle Arnie. The clipping is undated and does not show the name of the publication.

Former Dewsbury Scholar Killed in Action

It is with regret that we announce the receipt of the news of the death in action of Pte. Arnold Balmford (22), Duke of Wellington's Regiment (son of Mr and Mrs John A. Balmford, of Stonegarth, Halifax Old Road, Huddersfield, formerly of Dewsbury). Pte. Balmford will be remembered by many as a boy attending Carlton Road Board School up to 1908. He afterwards attended the Huddersfield Technical School, passing the matriculation examination, and he finished his education with twelve months at the Ecole Central Technique, Brussels. He was a good musician and gave promise of developing into a very fine bass vocalist, in which sphere he would probably have found his vocation. While in France with his regiment, speaking French exceedingly well, he made many friends very readily, and he had undertaken to sing the solo on Palm Sunday in the village church of Oisemont.

Unfortunately, he was prevented from doing this by his regiment being moved forward the day before. Pte. Balmford was well known in Dewsbury amongst some of the younger generation, as he had kept up his associations with his old schoolmates, many of whom are serving with the Colours. Much sympathy will be extended to Mr and Mrs Balmford in their sad bereavement.

Arnie is buried at the Arras Memorial in Arras, Departement du Pas-de-Calais, Nord-Pas-de-Calais, France.